MORNINGS & EVENINGS OF GRACE

LARGE PRINT WORD SEARCH

CHARLES H. SPURGEON

SEEKERS OF THE WORD

WHITAKER HOUSE

Publisher's note:
This book contains word searches based on selected readings from Charles Spurgeon's *Morning and Evening*. Spurgeon's original text has been lightly edited for the modern reader. Words, expressions, and sentence structure have been updated for clarity and readability, while retaining the entirety of Spurgeon's original writings.

All Scripture quotations are taken from the King James Version (KJV) of the Holy Bible.

Mornings & Evenings of Grace Large Print Word Search
100 Puzzles from the Timeless Christian Classic

ISBN: 979-8-88769-102-2

Printed in Colombia

© 2024 by Whitaker House

Whitaker House
1030 Hunt Valley Circle
New Kensington, PA 15068
www.whitakerhouse.com

1 2 3 4 5 6 7 8 9 10 11 ⨆ 31 30 29 28 27 26 25 24

DAY 1

Morning

*Grow in grace, and in the knowledge of our Lord
and Saviour Jesus Christ.*
—2 Peter 3:18

"*Grow in grace*"—not in one grace only, but in all grace. Grow in that root-grace, faith. Believe the promises more firmly than you have before. Let faith increase in fullness, constancy, and simplicity. Grow also in *love*. Ask that your love may become extended, more intense, more practical, influencing every thought, word, and deed. Grow likewise in *humility*. Seek to lie very low, and know more of your own nothingness. As you grow downward in humility, seek also to grow upward—having nearer approaches to God in prayer and more intimate fellowship with Jesus. May God the Holy Spirit enable you to "*grow…in the knowledge of our Lord and Saviour.*" He who does not grow in the knowledge of Jesus refuses to be blessed. To know Him is "*life eternal*" (John 17:3), and to advance in the knowledge of Him is to increase in happiness. He who does not long to know more of Christ knows nothing of Him yet. Whoever has sipped this wine will thirst for more, for although Christ satisfies, yet it is such a satisfaction that the appetite is not satiated, but whetted. If you know the love of Jesus, then, "*as the hart panteth after the water brooks*" (Ps. 42:1), so will you pant after deeper depths of His love. If you do not desire to know Him better, then you do not love Him, for love always cries, "Nearer, nearer." Absence from Christ is hell, but the presence of Jesus is heaven. Do not rest content, then, without an increasing acquaintance with Jesus. Seek to know more of Him in His divine nature, in His human relationship, in His finished work, in His death, in His resurrection, in His present glorious intercession, and in His future royal advent. Abide close to the cross, and search the mystery of His wounds. An increase of love for Jesus, and a more perfect apprehension of His love for us, is one of the best tests of growth in grace.

```
M A D Y D W K G J L X V Q E V R F Z F B
X P W W Y V D Z K W V P H L W I Y L E X
L P D I T L X M I K O H R Z M V V O L P
G R W J C Z N S I M P L I C I T Y S L R
Q E H N O O L B H J F M M U A P L I O A
H H E H U Z N O L K G R D A N O E P W C
U E T U A S R S C D W U N B G Y N P S T
M N T M R L B I T F M C Z S R S O E H I
G S E I Z S A T I A T E D E O M O D I C
I I D L Z D S G K N O O N W S B L P A
V O X I C J I Q X J T C H C S N K W M L
V N C T V B C A X J P N Y E A K E E X M
E I O Y I N T E N S E C M M T T N X F M
K D R E F M G M B K T K C K I C U T M M
W T V H M H B N L J G Y A J S F L E E Y
K N E A R E R G R A C E Y Z F E R N I G
B C R O K W J R X T Q M X A I G Z D I E
S A V I O R L E P R O M I S E S G E Y I
M Y S T E R Y N G B V Z G P S T L D V I
O W K L K K F U L L N E S S P M C V L Q
```

GRACE	GROW	SAVIOR	PROMISES
FULLNESS	CONSTANCY	SIMPLICITY	EXTENDED
INTENSE	PRACTICAL	HUMILITY	FELLOWSHIP
SIPPED	SATISFIES	SATIATED	WHETTED
NEARER	ABSENCE	MYSTERY	APPREHENSION

Evening

And Joseph knew his brethren, but they knew not him.
—Genesis 42:8

This morning our prayer went forth for growth in grace and in the knowledge of our Lord Jesus; it may be well tonight to consider a related topic, namely, our heavenly Joseph's knowledge of us. This knowledge was most blessedly perfect long before we had the slightest knowledge of Him. *"Thine eyes did see my substance, yet being unperfect; and in thy book all my members were written,…when as yet there was none of them"* (Ps. 139:16). Before we existed in the world, we existed in His heart. When we were enemies to Him, He knew us, with our misery, our foolishness, and our wickedness. When we wept bitterly in despairing repentance and viewed Him as only a judge and a ruler, He viewed us as His well-beloved brethren, and His heart yearned toward us. He never mistook His chosen, but always beheld them as objects of His infinite affection. *"The Lord knoweth them that are his"* (2 Tim. 2:19) is as true of the prodigals who are feeding swine as of the children who sit at the table. But, alas, we did not know our Royal Brother, and out of this ignorance grew a host of sins. We withheld our hearts from Him and allowed Him no entrance to our love. We mistrusted Him and gave no credit to His words. We rebelled against Him and paid Him no loving homage. The *"Sun of righteousness"* (Mal. 4:2) shone forth, and we could not see Him. Heaven came down to earth, and earth perceived it not. Let God be praised, for those days are over for us; yet even now we know but little of Jesus compared with what He knows of us. We have but begun to study Him, but He knows us completely. It is a blessed circumstance that the ignorance is not on His side, for then it would be a hopeless case for us. He will not say to us, *"I never knew you"* (Matt. 7:23). He will confess our names in the day of His appearing; meanwhile, He will manifest Himself to us as He does not to the world.

```
Y R N E C C O N F E S S U W X R H J J G
G S L S U B S T A N C E E W C O E V B I
C Y U K K B P A J C R P N F J Y A E F Y
U R S N B K B E F Y R P E A S A R N I T
K Z S K O L M R T Y A R M H Q L T T D H
Q N B W I F E B E C K F I O X B O R H R
N H O A O M R S V T G O E M L R K A C G
K P E W M I U I S Q H Q S A N O X N G A
S G J J L A L Y G E Z R Q G B T L C W P
X W G V M E N Y O H D W E E U H F E I P
G U I M S S D I T G T L F N I E O P G E
N E C N N W W G F H L E Y C A R B L N A
J B C C E T Y V E E J F O W W R W N O R
V I H O P E L E S S C S U M E P B R I
L P R O D I G A L S G T A P S Y P H A N
X M K A L H M D I U H C O S F N M Q N G
B D E O V W T R I O B D K R E B E B C P
C O M P L E T E L Y E X I S T E D S E G
C Y T W P X Y T C B V C S O O I I B S L
K Y J W S J L Z M R R N E J O S E P H T
```

JOSEPH	BRETHREN	KNOWLEDGE	BLESSEDLY
SUBSTANCE	EXISTED	HEART	ENEMIES
PRODIGALS	SWINE	ROYAL BROTHER	HOMAGE
SUN OF RIGHTEOUSNESS	COMPLETELY	IGNORANCE	HOPELESS
CONFESS	APPEARING	MANIFEST	ENTRANCE

Morning

*And God saw the light, that it was good: and God
divided the light from the darkness.*
—Genesis 1:4

Light might well be good, since it sprang from that command of goodness, *"Let there be light"* (Gen. 1:3). We who enjoy it should be more grateful for it than we are and see more of God *in* it and *by* it. *Physical* light was said by Solomon to be sweet, but *gospel* light is infinitely more precious, for it reveals eternal things and ministers to our immortal natures. When the Holy Spirit gives us spiritual light and opens our eyes to behold *"the glory of God in the face of Jesus Christ"* (2 Cor. 4:6), then we also behold sin in its true colors, and ourselves in our real position. We see the Most Holy God as He reveals Himself, the plan of mercy as He offers it, and the world to come as the Word describes it. Spiritual light has many beams and prismatic colors, but whether they are knowledge, joy, holiness, or life, they are all divinely good. If the light received is thus good, what must the essential Light be, and how glorious must the place where He reveals Himself be! O Lord, since light is so good, give us more of it, and more of Yourself, the true Light. No sooner is there a good thing in the world than a division is necessary. Light and darkness have no communion. God has divided them; let us not mistake them. Sons of light must not have fellowship with deeds, doctrines, or deceits of darkness. The children of the day must be sober, honest, and bold in their Lord's work, leaving the works of darkness to those who will dwell in it forever. Our churches should by discipline divide the light from the darkness, and we should by our distinct separation from the world do the same. In our judgments, actions, relationships, teaching, and listening, we must discern between the precious and the vile, and maintain the great distinction that the Lord made on the world's first day. O Lord Jesus, be our Light throughout the whole of this day, for Your light is the light of men.

```
Y T V Q O C G U M R Y Z B B Q X O P Q D
O V U M H C W P P E V R E V E A L S P I
V Y M O S T H O L Y R C L G Z R M I L V
T H P W D Z D A F I L C C N H B N V S I
A Q O B T Y L A B M D J Y M B Q R P O D
S E S L Q H N I X S E D K X X P M R L E
Z U I A F T D P N K E K P Z O H V E O D
D I T O B Y L L D F D B X M J Y L C M N
E M I R G Z L T B M S R Y A Q S A I O G
C T O N U O U V E Y X W G D I I Y O N D
E E N P F E O A Z G V H L O H C T U I N
I X G W A I C D C G Q G O C S A L S L J
T K U E S J N O O H Z W R T T L W K V M
S F O R O X V I L D N H I R D S N H N L
A G Y K J J R Q T O D W O I U E I G A H
K V M F S N U C D E R O U N B M M I H D
V L G R A T E F U L L S S E O D G A N C
U S P I R I T U A L J Y W S L I G H T C
U D A R K N E S S S O Y C D Z L V T D B
G L Q I X D E S S E N T I A L C X Q C K
```

LIGHT	DARKNESS	DIVIDED	GOOD
GRATEFUL	PHYSICAL	SOLOMON	INFINITELY
PRECIOUS	TRUE COLORS	POSITION	MOST HOLY
REVEALS	MERCY	SPIRITUAL	ESSENTIAL
GLORIOUS	DEEDS	DOCTRINES	DECEITS

Evening

And God saw the light.
—Genesis 1:4

This morning we noticed the goodness of the light, and the Lord's dividing it from the darkness. We now note the special eye that the Lord had for the light: *"God saw the light."* He looked at it with satisfaction, gazed on it with pleasure, and saw that it *"was good"* (Gen. 1:4). If the Lord has given you light, dear reader, He looks on that light with special interest, not only because it is dear to Him as His own handiwork, but also because it is like Himself, for *"God is light"* (1 John 1:5). It is pleasant to the believer to know that God's eye is thus tenderly observant of that work of grace that He has begun in him. He never loses sight of the treasure that He has placed in our earthen vessels. Sometimes we cannot see the light, but God always sees the light, and that is much better than our seeing it. Better for the judge to see my innocence than for me to think I see it. It is very comfortable for me to know that I am one of God's people; but whether I know it or not, if the Lord knows it, I am still safe. This is the foundation: *"The Lord knoweth them that are his"* (2 Tim. 2:19). You may be sighing and groaning because of inbred sin and mourning over your darkness, yet the Lord sees light in your heart, for He has put it there. All the cloudiness and gloom of your soul cannot conceal your light from His gracious eye. You may have sunk low in despondency and even despair, but if your soul has any longing toward Christ, and if you are seeking to rest in His finished work, God sees the light. He not only sees it, but also preserves it in you. *"I the Lord do keep it"* (Isa. 27:3). This is a precious thought to those who, after anxious watching and guarding of themselves, feel their own powerlessness to keep themselves. The light thus preserved by God's grace He will one day develop into the splendor of noonday and the fullness of glory. The light within is the dawn of the eternal day.

```
Y M N X P E M R S T M J C G N K I I Q O
O I P B R H H V G L K A U Z R E N N I V
J D L D E D A O Q I Z M Z D I W N T U R
V S E I S E B N P P P U O A G K O E F W
Q I A V E Z I F D R B U I S B E C R A F
B G S I R Y H R O I Q K X Q Y J E E H F
P H U D V D D Z A U W D J L S O N S D R
Z I R I E Q Q X B K N O H D L T C T E Z
D N E N D O G G U U T D R X Q X E E S X
R G D G G O O D N E S S A K F B D X P E
J Q K Z D N U A T B V H S T D C U P A J
S V I K O Q H F R Z L O Q I I V A S I N
F T P S P E C I A L L Q H Q Y O E Z R M
C V E S S E L S X W E L O N G I N G U C
E E A R T H E N G V J O K C L F V S Q F
W B Z N X J X I V S E A Z G A Z E D E H
C F D X U G R O A N I N G P H R S S S A
Z S A T I S F A C T I O N D B B R C Z Z
Y G G P G W E J O Q A B E L I E V E R G
Y C V X M V G O D S E Y E M F O C V R W
```

GOODNESS	DIVIDING	SATISFACTION	GAZED
PLEASURE	SPECIAL	INTEREST	HANDIWORK
BELIEVER	GOD'S EYE	EARTHEN	VESSELS
JUDGE	INNOCENCE	FOUNDATION	SIGHING
GROANING	DESPAIR	LONGING	PRESERVED

11

Morning

These have no root.
—Luke 8:13

My soul, examine yourself this morning in the light of today's text. You have received the Word with joy. Your feelings have been stirred, and a lively impression has been made. But remember: to receive the Word in your ears is one thing; to receive Jesus into your very soul is quite another. Superficial feeling is often joined to inward hardness of heart, and a lively impression of the Word is not always a lasting one. In the parable of the sower, the seed in one case fell on ground having a rocky bottom, covered over with a thin layer of earth. When the seed began to take root, its downward growth was hindered by the hard stone; therefore, it spent its strength in pushing its green shoot aloft as high as it could; but, having no inward moisture derived from root nourishment, it withered away. Is this my case? Have I been making a fair show in the flesh without having a corresponding inner life? Good growth takes place upward and downward at the same time. Am I rooted in sincere fidelity and love for Jesus? If my heart remains hardened and unfertilized by grace, the good seed may germinate for a season, but it must ultimately wither, for it cannot flourish on a rocky, unbroken, unsanctified heart. Let me dread a godliness as rapid in growth and as lacking in endurance as Jonah's gourd. Let me count the cost of being a follower of Jesus. Above all, let me feel the energy of His Holy Spirit, and then, I will possess an abiding and enduring seed in my soul. If my mind remains as stubborn as it was by nature, the sun of trial will scorch, and my hard heart will help to cast the heat the more terribly on the ill-covered seed. My faith will soon die, and my despair will be terrible; therefore, O heavenly Sower, plough me first, and then, cast the truth into me. Let me yield a bounteous harvest for You.

```
Q N I E E Y P H G X E E P T D T F H P P
L E O W F Q E M H R E P L X T T E S R H
P X D R U F N Q J N O V D Z C W E R O I
I I O C O C Q H M S Y W J P J Q L E C N
I Q W F E O F A S F G S T M Z G I C K D
I N N I H I T R U D P E E H T J N E Y E
Y C W Q T R W D M X S X R C O R G I B R
X C A A U E J N O E T F D M W U S V O E
B G R T R F B E R X I C D Q I N V E T D
J I D H Z D K S N A R A E N L N E D T M
H Z C W F E K S I M R A N O H F A W O V
U S C B V K U F N I E T G N H V F T M Q
U S C E C U W Y G N D U F S I R E U E U
L I V E L Y B J G E A H A R D E N E D I
C E W S U P E R F I C I A L C S O O E X
B N J E P M L Z M R H P T P J C E E J F
W J A S U N F E R T I L I Z E D W H X A
N H F H R D I M P R E S S I O N V D P K
E N D U R A N C E W J F L O U R I S H D
T A X Z Y C O J G N G N N A N K P P H Z
```

NO ROOT	EXAMINE	MORNING	FEELINGS
RECEIVED	STIRRED	LIVELY	IMPRESSION
SUPERFICIAL	INWARD	HARDNESS	ROCKY BOTTOM
DOWNWARD	GROWTH	HINDERED	HARDENED
UNFERTILIZED	GERMINATE	FLOURISH	ENDURANCE

Evening

I have prayed for thee, that thy faith fail not.
—Luke 22:32

How encouraging is the thought of the Redeemer's never-ceasing intercession for us. When we pray, He pleads for us; and when we are not praying, He is advocating our cause, and by His supplications shielding us from unseen dangers. Notice the word of comfort addressed to Peter: *"Simon, Simon, behold, Satan hath desired to have you, that he may sift you as wheat: but…"* (Luke 22:31–32). But what? "But go and pray for yourself"? That would be good advice, but that is not what is written. Neither did our Lord say, "But I will keep you watchful, and so you will be preserved." That, too, would be a great blessing. But no, He said, *"I have prayed for thee, that thy faith fail not."* We know little of what we owe to our Savior's prayers. When we reach the hilltops of heaven and look back on all the ways in which the Lord our God has led us, how we will praise Him who, before the eternal throne, undid the mischief that Satan was doing on earth! How we will thank Him because He never withheld His peace, but day and night He pointed to the wounds on His hands and carried our names on His breastplate! Even before Satan had begun to tempt, Jesus had forestalled him and entered a plea in heaven. Mercy outruns malice. Note that He did not say, "Satan hath sifted you; therefore, I will pray," but He said, *"Satan hath desired to have you."* He checked Satan even in his very desire and nipped it in the bud. He did not say, "But I have desired to pray for you." No, He said, "*'I have prayed for thee.'* I have done it already. I have gone to court and entered a counterplea even before an accusation is made." O Jesus, what a comfort it is that You have pleaded our cause against our unseen enemies, disarmed their mines, and unmasked their ambushes. This is a matter for joy, gratitude, hope, and confidence.

```
G F R O S U W A T C H F U L E B B V L D
A U R P R E S E R V E D W M G R A C X Y
P N Q A E A V A G R E S G I G E I O X H
C Z A D V I C E R F M U U S N A M U S X
P L E A D S Z R A P M P S C E S X N H I
X R G P U R E H T X X P A H V T A T I F
Y U V V V X V V I A W L P I E P C E E H
E E I C E E V R T B N I R E R L C R L I
K X O E Z Q P Z U T M C A F C A U P D E
X M D W M L Y W D P T A Y C E T S L I N
U J M K S K Y A E U A T E G A E A E N C
N W B B U Y K K M A F I D H S W T A G O
A D V O C A T I N G Q O U C I N I G C U
N D K N C Q P H E N R N M T N D O E J R
F Q F A I L N O T G A S P N G Z N N P A
Y I N T E R C E S S I O N A N J I M M G
T U H A K V I F X H I L L T O P S E B I
G E W Z R D H R Y G D M I E C K W F S N
Z L A X B T L T E C O N F I D E N C E G
E T E R N A L T H R O N E H H R N R Q X
```

PRAYED	FAIL NOT	ENCOURAGING	NEVER-CEASING
INTERCESSION	PLEADS	ADVOCATING	SUPPLICATIONS
SHIELDING	ADVICE	WATCHFUL	PRESERVED
HILLTOPS	MISCHIEF	ETERNAL THRONE	BREASTPLATE
COUNTERPLEA	ACCUSATION	GRATITUDE	CONFIDENCE

Morning

*He expounded unto them in all the scriptures
the things concerning himself.*
—Luke 24:27

The two disciples on the road to Emmaus had a most profitable journey. Their companion and teacher was the best of tutors, their interpreter one of a thousand, *"in whom are hid all the treasures of wisdom and knowledge"* (Col. 2:3). The Lord Jesus condescended to become a preacher of the Gospel, and He was not ashamed to exercise His calling before an audience of two persons; neither does He now refuse to become the teacher of even one. Let us court the company of so excellent an Instructor, for until He is *"made unto us wisdom"* (1 Cor. 1:30), we will never be *"wise unto salvation"* (2 Tim. 3:15). This unrivalled Tutor used as His textbook the Best of Books. Although able to reveal fresh truth, He preferred to expound the old. He knew by His omniscience what was the most instructive way of teaching, and by turning immediately to Moses and the prophets, He showed us that the surest road to wisdom is not speculating, reasoning, or reading human books, but meditating on the Word of God. The readiest way to be spiritually rich in heavenly knowledge is to dig in this mine of diamonds, to gather pearls from this heavenly sea. When Jesus Himself sought to enrich others, He dug in the quarry of Holy Scripture. The favored pair were led to consider the best of subjects, for Jesus *"expounded…the things concerning himself."* Here the diamond cut the diamond, and what could be more admirable? The Master of the house unlocked His own doors, conducted the guests to His table, and placed His own delicacies on it. He who hid the treasure in the field guided the searchers to it Himself. Our Lord would naturally discourse upon the sweetest of topics, and He could find none sweeter than His own person and work. With an eye to these truths, we should always search the Word. Oh, for grace to study the Bible with Jesus as both our Teacher and our Lesson!

```
G A W U R V S E D Y E C T E A C H E R Q
T T W V J O U R N E Y X H I S I B I Q A
P H T M S C R I P T U R E S T N Y Y W U
D Q O T E D Z X T L Y T S L W S F A S D
I L I U D R E A D I N G G K M T C O P I
A A T Z S C B H E X E X G Q S R J Q E E
V O I Y I A X I O A O N T U B U N C C N
G E X P O U N D E D O R L X X C C O U C
E X E C I S E D Q U Y C T T W T O N L E
M O S E S V S Y X U E N H H O I M C A U
E Z R Y F P R E A S O N I N G V P E T F
D N L E W G R F V A V C X J Z E A R I Q
I G H Q X D T O E P V A C S I Y N N N W
T U G C Q Y L F P W P G C I S C I I G U
A R W K O W Q N A H E Q Y F Q G O N H I
T D U D S E I T E R E D R E B O N G Y N
I T R E A S U R E S X T T J M P X W Z T
N O M N I S C I E N C E S A S U X M L A
G J X O P P R O F I T A B L E V R E N C
R V C L G T I N T E R P R E T E R Q R Y
```

EXPOUNDED	SCRIPTURES	CONCERNING	PROFITABLE
JOURNEY	COMPANION	TEACHER	INTERPRETER
THOUSAND	TREASURES	EXERCISE	AUDIENCE
OMNISCIENCE	INSTRUCTIVE	MOSES	PROPHETS
MEDITATING	SPECULATING	REASONING	READING

Evening

Son of man, What is the vine tree more than any tree, or than
a branch which is among the trees of the forest?
—Ezekiel 15:2

These words are for the humbling of God's people. They are called God's vine, but what are they by nature more than others? They, by God's goodness, have become fruitful, having been planted in a good soil. The Lord has trained them upon the walls of the sanctuary, and they bring forth fruit to His glory; but what are they without their God? What are they without the continual influence of the Spirit producing fruitfulness in them? Believer, learn to reject pride, seeing that you have no ground for it. Whatever you are, you have nothing to make you proud. The more you have, the more you are in debt to God; and you should not be proud of that which makes you a debtor. Consider your origin; look back to what you were. Consider what you would have been had it not been for divine grace. Look on yourself as you are now. Does not your conscience reproach you? Do not your thousand wanderings stand before you and tell you that you are unworthy to be called His child? And if He has made you anything, are you not taught thereby that it is grace that has changed you? Great believer, you would have been a great sinner if God had not transformed you. O you who are valiant for truth, you would have been as valiant for error if grace had not laid hold of you. Therefore, be not proud, though you have a large estate, that is, a wide domain of grace. Once, you did not have a single thing to call your own except your sin and misery. Oh, strange infatuation, that you, who have borrowed everything, would think of exalting yourself! You are a poor pensioner dependent on the bounty of your Savior; you are one who has a life that dies without fresh streams of life from Jesus, and yet you are still proud! Shame on you, O lowly heart!

```
R  W  O  C  C  Q  I  J  S  V  S  Z  A  A  G  W  S  V  N  B
Y  V  M  Q  E  J  C  Q  F  Y  N  B  F  M  O  C  O  A  Q  J
Q  F  N  S  K  N  R  D  L  S  X  X  O  T  O  O  N  L  A  P
Q  B  Y  A  Q  G  T  I  G  N  S  S  R  R  D  N  O  I  T  R
B  W  M  I  M  L  T  N  Y  I  A  L  E  A  N  S  F  A  H  O
E  R  A  R  E  Q  Z  M  J  F  N  Z  S  I  E  C  M  N  U  D
C  M  A  N  D  T  V  Q  O  Z  C  X  T  N  S  I  A  T  M  U
L  R  L  N  D  L  Y  G  H  N  T  A  N  E  S  E  N  B  B  C
D  L  H  U  C  E  W  X  K  P  U  P  U  D  C  N  S  I  L  I
F  N  D  W  B  H  R  Z  P  L  A  N  T  E  D  C  B  N  I  N
R  N  G  B  G  I  W  I  L  O  R  V  V  O  T  E  O  F  N  G
U  B  G  Y  P  S  S  S  N  Q  Y  E  I  E  S  A  L  L  G  H
I  O  Z  F  O  C  F  I  Q  G  Q  N  N  G  N  H  Z  U  B  U
T  U  V  U  P  H  G  F  J  H  S  M  E  X  P  T  E  E  R  E
F  N  I  W  R  I  D  L  U  T  L  W  T  Y  E  J  C  N  A  D
U  T  U  P  V  L  T  L  L  Q  E  V  R  X  S  A  I  C  Y  H
L  Y  T  X  N  D  G  G  Y  L  C  U  E  E  H  B  E  E  V  S
I  Q  O  E  J  N  A  T  U  R  E  T  E  B  P  M  J  H  W  K
I  G  O  O  D  S  O  I  L  M  U  R  P  Y  X  G  Y  V  U  J
P  O  R  I  G  I  N  F  M  Q  G  A  D  H  S  B  A  S  I  O
```

SON OF MAN	VINE TREE	BRANCH	FOREST
HUMBLING	NATURE	GOODNESS	FRUITFUL
PLANTED	GOOD SOIL	TRAINED	SANCTUARY
INFLUENCE	PRODUCING	ORIGIN	CONSCIENCE
WANDERINGS	HIS CHILD	VALIANT	BOUNTY

Morning

Do we then make void the law through faith?
God forbid: yea, we establish the law.
—Romans 3:31

When the believer is adopted into the Lord's family, his relationship to Old Adam and the law ceases at once; but then he is under a new rule and a new covenant. Believer, you are God's child. It is your first duty to obey your heavenly Father. You have nothing to do with a servile spirit: you are not a slave but a child. And now, inasmuch as you are a beloved child, you are bound to obey your Father's faintest wish, the least intimation of His will. Does He bid you to fulfill a sacred ordinance? It is at your peril that you neglect it, for you will be disobeying your Father. Does He command you to seek the image of Jesus? Is it not your joy to do so? Does Jesus tell you, *"Be ye therefore perfect, even as your Father which is in heaven is perfect"* (Matt. 5:48)? Then not because the law commands, but because your Savior directs, you will labor to be perfect in holiness. Does He bid His saints to love one another? Do it, not because the law says, *"Love thy neighbour"* (Lev. 19:18), but because Jesus says, *"If ye love me, keep my commandments"* (John 14:15). This is the commandment that He has given to you, *"That ye love one another"* (John 13:34). Are you told to give to the poor? Do it, not because charity is a burden that you dare not shirk, but because Jesus teaches, *"Give to every man that asketh of thee"* (Luke 6:30). Does the Word say, "Love God with all your heart"? (See Deuteronomy 6:5.) Look at the commandment and reply, "Ah, commandment, Christ has fulfilled you already. I have no need, therefore, to fulfill you for my salvation, but I rejoice to yield obedience to you because God is my Father now, and He has a claim on me that I would not dispute." May the Holy Spirit make your heart obedient to the constraining power of Christ's love, so that your prayer may be, *"Make me to go in the path of thy commandments; for therein do I delight"* (Ps. 119:35). Grace is the mother and nurse of holiness, and not the apologist of sin.

```
L M B U E O B E D I E N C E A H O H X B
S Q I E N S I N T I M A T I O N K O H E
P B X J R E T K R R T X K V F K V L O L
K R Z H I W W A B N P X G J M M H I E O
G U Y F M W S R B D W N X D T G Z N T V
J I U E A O T Z U L Z I P Z O T R E M E
M S R Q G F H U H L I K K W L W E S J D
E A Y F E V L R Q A E S E W D U L S Z C
E K Z M O C X C M E Y B H E A N A D B H
A M F U L F I L L E D X P M D Z T O O I
C O V E N A N T L Q T O S A A U I G S L
C C H A R I T Y E S M P Z K M N O I R D
A C O M M A N D X C E E M E H L N G V W
K O G R A X E E Y B D R X V P G S H J I
Z D D A V V W U L N W F V O L Q H D G D
F O R D I N A N C E H E S I S M I K J G
M J Y J A Z R U C C N C L D L Q P V P W
C O N T R A I N I N G T V W B E F R T S
H D W V E L F N Q X S A L V A T I O N K
A D O P T E D N S F J J U F R D B Z N C
```

MAKE VOID	ESTABLISH	ADOPTED	RELATIONSHIP
OLD ADAM	NEW RULE	COVENANT	SERVILE
BELOVED CHILD	INTIMATION	ORDINANCE	COMMAND
IMAGE	PERFECT	HOLINESS	CHARITY
FULFILLED	SALVATION	OBEDIENCE	CONSTRAINING

21

Evening

And of his fulness have all we received.
—John 1:16

These words tell us that there is a fullness in Christ. There is a fullness of essential deity and a fullness of perfect manhood, for *"in him dwelleth all the fulness of the Godhead bodily"* (Col. 2:9). There is a fullness of atoning efficacy in His blood, for *"the blood of Jesus Christ his Son cleanseth us from all sin"* (1 John 1:7). There is a fullness of justifying righteousness in His life, for *"there is therefore now no condemnation to them which are in Christ Jesus"* (Rom. 8:1). There is a fullness of divine prevalence in His plea, for *"he is able also to save them to the uttermost that come unto God by him, seeing he ever liveth to make intercession for them"* (Heb. 7:25). There is a fullness of victory in His death, for through death He destroyed *"him that had the power of death, that is, the devil"* (Heb. 2:14). There is a fullness of efficacy in His resurrection from the dead, for by it we are *"begotten…again unto a lively hope"* (1 Pet. 1:3). There is a fullness of triumph in His ascension, for when He *"ascended on high, [He] led captivity captive…[and] received gifts for men"* (Ps. 68:18). (See also, Ephesians 4:8.) There is a fullness of blessings of every sort and shape: a fullness of grace to pardon, of grace to regenerate, of grace to sanctify, of grace to preserve, and of grace to perfect. There is a fullness at all times: a fullness of comfort in affliction, a fullness of guidance in prosperity. There is a fullness of every divine attribute: of wisdom, of power, of love. This fullness of blessings is impossible to survey, much less to explore. *"It pleased the Father that in him should all fulness dwell"* (Col. 1:19). Oh, what a fullness this must be of which all receive! Fullness, indeed, there must be when the stream is always flowing, and yet the well springs up as free, as rich, as full as ever. Come, believer, and find all your needs supplied. Ask largely, and you will receive largely, for this fullness is inexhaustible; it is stored up where all the needy may reach it—in Jesus, Immanuel, *"God with us"* (Matt. 1:23).

```
N T Z I X W Z N W M M C U E B S P K F W
P Q R I G H T E O U S N E S S C O G U O
S D E I T Y O P N T J P J S L T O G L S
H B L E S S I N G S R A N E I T L G L H
B J Y E S N R B S D W R P N C Z T V N J
V E H D F I O E K J J D M T P Q R X E U
Y W G O K F R X C Q O O B I H X I B S S
P P U O X N I A V E A N H A S X U G S T
G R M R T U S C B V I S Y L G Z M S V I
W R E V I T A A A I B V C K Z M P C E F
C K S S O O E U T C R L E E Z L H C B Y
Q H Y I E P W N Y T Y W N D N X N J M I
O H W H G R C M S O O D W J Z S F Q V N
C K K B E S V S O R J Y U Y M U I H W G
Z U J C T Y W E K Y I B N B D R N O S E
T L R E S U R R E C T I O N O I U I N N
S A N C T I F Y U R E G E N E R A T E W
U S Y J A T O N I N G W I G C D G A N K
M U H R V V M F S P H D I V I N E U S J
P S E Z R W E R Q P R E V A L E N C E U
```

FULLNESS	RECEIVED	ESSENTIAL	DEITY
ATONING	EFFICACY	JUSTIFYING	RIGHTEOUSNESS
DIVINE	PREVALENCE	VICTORY	BEGOTTEN
RESURRECTION	TRIUMPH	ASCENSION	BLESSINGS
PARDON	REGENERATE	SANCTIFY	PRESERVE

Morning

In whom also we have obtained an inheritance.
—Ephesians 1:11

When Jesus gave Himself for us, He gave us all the rights and privileges that are in Him. Although, as eternal God, He has essential rights to which no creature may venture to claim, as Jesus, the Mediator, the federal Head of the covenant of grace, He now has no heritage apart from us. All the glorious consequences of His obedience unto death are the joint riches of all who are in Him and on whose behalf He accomplished the divine will. Note that He entered into glory, but not for Himself alone, for it is written, *"Whither the forerunner is **for us** entered"* (Heb. 6:20, emphasis added). Does He stand in the presence of God? He appears *"in the presence of God **for us**"* (Heb. 9:24, emphasis added). Consider this, believer: you have no right to heaven in yourself; your right lies in Christ. If you are pardoned, it is through His blood. If you are justified, it is through His righteousness. If you are sanctified, it is because you are in Jesus, *"who of God is made unto* [you] *…sanctification"* (1 Cor. 1:30). If you will be kept from falling, it will be because you are preserved in Christ Jesus; and if you are perfected at the last, it will be because you are *"complete in him"* (Col. 2:10). Thus Jesus is magnified, for all is in Him and by Him. The inheritance is made certain to us, for it is obtained in Him, and each blessing is sweeter—even heaven itself the brighter—because it is Jesus our Beloved *"in whom also we have obtained"* all. Where is the person who can estimate our divine portion? Weigh the riches of Christ and His treasure; then try to count the treasures that belong to the saints. Reach the bottom of Christ's sea of joy; then hope to understand the bliss *"which God hath prepared for them that love him"* (1 Cor. 2:9). Hurdle the boundaries of Christ's possessions; then dream of a limit to the fair inheritance of the elect. *"All things are yours;…ye are Christ's; and Christ is God's"* (1 Cor. 3:21, 23).

```
L T P G T E W V S L M Z C W R U D L G O
A E F A L U B C R E A T U R E V K F L K
Q G L O R L L P K C W R P Y Y K V O O P
H V P N B D D Y E H V M R J Q P E R R V
E Q V B C T O B T U U T E T O R N E I D
R Q I W Y V A N Z J B W S W B I T R O F
I E O N C F F I E N G V E U E V U U U J
T J X X H L D Z N D I I N N D I R N S D
A X H Y Y E A F U E A J C L I L E N L H
G F R N H P R I K X D Q E Z E E U E R E
E O Y A U J Y I M Y K D W W N G Q R Z H
S T H V I C G W T G R Y Q H C E F M A X
S I E B L P L I U A O P G E E S Q E L J
E S C O N S E Q U E N C E S D X P M F G
N P R E S E R V E D F C J O N J G R V M
T Y A C C O M P L I S H E D E U Y G O X
I K D B S D P H P A X E T E R N A L A N
A K U N T O D E A T H O U N P P L B F L
L U V O O M M X J Y R C R I G H T S K T
W I E J E E I D I V I N E W I L L L C W
```

OBTAINED	INHERITANCE	RIGHTS	PRIVILEGES
ETERNAL	ESSENTIAL	CREATURE	VENTURE
CLAIM	HERITAGE	GLORIOUS	CONSEQUENCES
OBEDIENCE	UNTO DEATH	ACCOMPLISHED	DIVINE WILL
FORERUNNER	PRESENCE	PARDONED	PRESERVED

Evening

The Lord Our Righteousness.
—Jeremiah 23:6

It will always give a Christian the greatest calm, quiet, ease, and peace to think of the perfect righteousness of Christ. How often are the saints of God downcast and sad! I do not think they should be. I do not think they would be if they could always see their perfection in Christ. Some are always talking about corruption, the depravity of the heart, and the innate evil of the soul. These things are quite true, but why not go a little further and remember that we are *"perfect in Christ Jesus"* (Col. 1:28)? It is no wonder that those who are dwelling on their own corruption should wear such downcast looks; but surely, if we call to mind that *"Christ Jesus…is made unto us…righteousness"* (1 Cor. 1:30), we will be of good cheer. Even though distresses afflict me and Satan assaults me; even though there may be many things to be experienced before I get to heaven, these things are done for me in the covenant of divine grace. Nothing is lacking in my Lord! Christ has done it all! On the cross, He said, *"It is finished"* (John 19:30), and if it is finished, then I am complete in Him and can *"rejoice with joy unspeakable and full of glory"* (1 Pet. 1:8). *"Not having mine own righteousness, which is of the law, but that which is through the faith of Christ, the righteousness which is of God by faith"* (Phil. 3:9). You will not find on this side of heaven a holier people than those who receive into their hearts the doctrine of Christ's righteousness. When the believer says, "I live in Christ alone. I rest solely on Him for salvation; and I believe that, however unworthy, I am still saved in Jesus," then there rises up as a motive of gratitude these thoughts: "Will I not live for Christ? Will I not love Him and serve Him, seeing that I am saved by His merits?" *"The love of Christ constraineth us…that they which live should not henceforth live unto themselves, but unto him which died for them"* (2 Cor. 5:14–15). If we are saved by imputed righteousness, we will greatly value imparted righteousness.

```
J  R  C  X  X  M  J  Y  I  N  V  C  T  H  E  L  O  R  D  P
C  J  Z  X  T  C  O  V  R  G  O  O  D  C  H  E  E  R  L  P
Z  L  U  C  P  G  V  T  O  M  B  D  Y  S  A  E  W  I  A  H
A  F  O  I  K  Y  F  Q  I  T  X  V  I  G  Y  N  X  N  K  V
C  S  C  A  L  M  D  S  A  V  L  G  D  R  W  B  N  D  J  I
N  P  D  X  U  L  V  Q  K  Y  E  K  F  E  F  P  Q  I  Z  M
B  K  S  F  G  S  P  W  U  D  R  X  O  A  N  Y  W  E  R  P
S  A  L  V  A  T  I  O  N  I  D  L  Z  T  I  H  H  X  Y  U
P  E  R  F  E  C  T  S  F  K  E  I  E  E  P  Z  O  P  F  T
W  D  I  G  V  B  H  V  Z  A  G  T  A  S  Z  O  L  E  G  E
H  J  K  G  N  I  M  P  A  R  T  E  D  T  D  K  I  R  O  D
R  D  F  G  R  L  C  H  R  I  S  T  A  L  O  N  E  I  W  J
L  C  O  V  E  N  A  N  T  S  P  G  W  N  F  B  R  E  T  V
C  V  O  Y  I  V  I  Y  M  M  Y  W  L  D  B  I  O  N  P  P
O  Q  Y  G  E  H  S  X  N  Q  M  O  A  E  S  N  E  C  S  E
X  O  G  A  N  V  A  J  G  R  A  T  I  T  U  D  E  E  B  A
N  O  T  R  I  G  H  T  E  O  U  S  N  E  S  S  H  D  D  C
Y  S  O  J  F  I  Q  C  S  X  S  S  F  P  W  S  M  L  B  E
Y  R  T  K  A  V  G  X  D  O  W  N  C  A  S  T  S  J  I  I
F  H  E  K  Y  E  E  Y  K  R  V  A  L  U  E  A  S  E  N  U
```

THE LORD	RIGHTEOUSNESS	GREATEST	CALM
QUIET	EASE	PEACE	PERFECT
DOWNCAST	GOOD CHEER	EXPERIENCED	COVENANT
HOLIER	CHRIST ALONE	SALVATION	MOTIVE
GRATITUDE	IMPUTED	IMPARTED	VALUE

27

Morning

Without shedding of blood is no remission.
—Hebrews 9:22

This is the voice of unalterable truth. In none of the Jewish ceremonies were sins, even typically, removed without the shedding of blood. In no case, by no means, can sin be pardoned without atonement. It is clear, then, that there is no hope for me apart from Christ; for there is no other shedding of blood than His that is worth a thought as an atonement for sin. Am I, then, believing in Him? Is the blood of His atonement truly applied to my soul? All men are equal as to their need of Him. Even if we are moral, generous, amiable, or patriotic, the rule will not be altered to make an exception for us. Sin will yield to nothing less potent than the blood of Him whom God has set forth as a propitiation. What a blessing that there is the one way of pardon! Why should we seek another? Persons of merely formal religion cannot understand how we can rejoice that all our sins are forgiven for Christ's sake. Their works, prayers, and ceremonies give them very little comfort. It is good that they are uneasy, for they are neglecting the one great salvation and endeavoring to get remission without blood. My soul, take the time to consider that the justice of God is obligated to punish sin. See that punishment executed on your Lord Jesus and fall down in humble joy. Kiss the dear feet of Him whose blood has made atonement for you. It is in vain when the conscience is aroused to fly to feelings and evidences for comfort: we learned this habit in the Egypt of our legal bondage. The only restorative for a guilty conscience is a sight of Jesus suffering on the cross. *"The blood is the life"* (Deut. 12:23) says the Levitical law, and let us rest assured that it is the life of faith and joy and every other holy grace.

Oh, how sweet to view the flowing
    Of my Savior's precious blood;
With divine assurance knowing
    He has made my peace with God.

```
N K G A H B P V L F Y Z X P F U V T I Y
D N C R Y U V T U L W A O Q T W B Z W R
I W A I P O P W Y B S U L Q B W L T U L
W I T H O U T F O R G I V E N B O A O L
A P R O P I T I A T I O N W G H O S B O
P M A A A T P I X N G K V J M V D S O S
P L P P R A Y E R S N V O I C E N U N Z
L E H O V U F L O F V P T Y Y F E R D A
I V C E R E M O N I E S P T K Y G A A T
E I F E G P A R D O N E D M Y R L N G T
D T R F F G I X J A B O D G N E E C E L
P I X R W J L V W G J W K N B M C E X E
I C T A E A V L T R F A I H N I T W V U
B A F E U N A L T E R A B L E S I N K C
O L G O B W Y V O Y H H U U Z S N T P A
A O E U A L N F P O H J U E D I G R Z V
H S H I L T W O R K S Y L W E O V U W P
A T O N E M E N T D R C Z P Y N A T N T
I A E K U L E N K V V Y N Q Q I C H E D
S H E D D I N G E N D E A V O R I N G M
```

WITHOUT	SHEDDING	BLOOD	REMISSION
VOICE	UNALTERABLE	TRUTH	CEREMONIES
PARDONED	ATONEMENT	APPLIED	PROPITIATION
WORKS	PRAYERS	LEVITICAL	FORGIVEN
NEGLECTING	ENDEAVORING	BONDAGE	ASSURANCE

DAY 7

Evening

And these are ancient things.
—1 Chronicles 4:22

These things are not as ancient as those precious things that delight our souls. Let us for a moment recall them, recounting them as misers delight in calculating the worth of their gold. The sovereign choice of the Father, by which He elected us to eternal life, before *"the earth was"* (Prov. 8:23), is a matter of vast antiquity, since no date can be conceived for it in the mind of man. We were *"chosen…in him before the foundation of the world"* (Eph. 1:4). Everlasting love went with the choice, for it was not a mere act of divine will by which we were set apart, but divine affection was also involved. The Father loved us in and from the beginning. Here is a theme for daily contemplation. The eternal purpose to redeem us from our foreseen ruin, to cleanse and sanctify us, and, at last, to glorify us was of infinite antiquity; it runs side by side with immutable love and absolute sovereignty. The covenant is always described as being everlasting, and Jesus, the second party in it, was actively involved from the start. He struck hands in sacred suretyship long before the first of the stars began to shine, and it was in Him that the elect were ordained to eternal life. Thus in the divine purpose a most blessed covenant union was established between the Son of God and His elect people, which will remain as the foundation of their safety when time will be no more. Is it not well to be conversant with these ancient things? Is it not shameful that they should be so much neglected and even rejected by the majority of believers? If they knew more of their own sin, would they not be more ready to adore His amazing grace? Let us both admire and adore Him tonight, as we sing,

A monument of grace,
　A sinner saved by blood!
The streams of love I trace
　Up to the Fountain, God;
And in His sacred bosom see
　Eternal thoughts of love to me.

```
U O N S W P W Q L T H K P U N I O N D M
Z E V E R L A S T I N G C V B C R I E C
Y G W Q B H L F M U N Q I O O W D C L C
G R E T E R N A L P U R P O S E I A I O
D C C N N X Y O T R N Z M Y T G V L G N
Q W W C D P F B Z S W Z D A M P I C H T
E O N M A F F E C T I O N Y S L N U T E
F V C O R T M B F H V H D P W A E L V M
Z F O A B G J D S Y O W B X F T W A L P
O O N Z P N L P Z I O I S M R I I T A L
F U C M C F C I R I J D C T E D L I C A
Y N E N K S T K W E X A C E C Y L N L T
L D I A G X L O B P C K R D A O J G E I
F A V A N C I E N T K I J H L T Q C A O
S T E R X X G I C G N P O K L V L C N N
R I D E S O V E R E I G N U A O J M S N
Q O Y S E R O C D L L B R R S T K X E L
E N W O R T H I E F C G E L E C T E D I
Q P P X E W A N T I Q U I T Y M A B S Z
S Z I M V E X S A N C T I F Y F A N L G
```

ANCIENT	PRECIOUS	DELIGHT	RECALL
CALCULATING	WORTH	SOVEREIGN	CHOICE
ELECTED	ANTIQUITY	CONCEIVED	FOUNDATION
EVERLASTING	DIVINE WILL	AFFECTION	CONTEMPLATION
ETERNAL PURPOSE	CLEANSE	SANCTIFY	UNION

Morning

Your refuge from the avenger of blood.
—Joshua 20:3

It is said that in the land of Canaan, cities of refuge were set up so that any man might reach one of them within half a day at the most. Likewise, the word of our salvation is near to us. Jesus is a present Savior, and the distance to Him is short. It requires only a simple renunciation of our own merit and a laying hold of Jesus to be our all in all. With regard to the roads leading to the cities of refuge, we are told that they were carefully preserved. Every river was bridged and every obstruction removed, so that the man who fled might find an easy passage to safety. Once a year the elders went along the roads and saw to their order, so that nothing might impede the flight of anyone or cause him, through delay, to be overtaken and slain. How graciously do the promises of the Gospel remove stumbling blocks from our paths! Wherever there were hidden roads or turns, there were signs placed, with this inscription on them: "To the city of refuge!" This is a picture of the road to Christ Jesus. It is no roundabout road of the law. It does not involve obeying endless rules; it is a straight road: "Believe and live." (See John 20:31.) It is a road so hard that no self-righteous man can ever tread it, but so easy that every sinner, who knows himself to be a sinner, may by it find his way to heaven. No sooner did the manslayer reach the outskirts of the city than he was safe. It was not necessary for him to pass far within the walls, for the suburbs themselves were sufficient protection. Learn that if you touch just the hem of Christ's garment, you will be made whole; if you will only lay hold on him with *"faith as a grain of mustard seed"* (Matt. 17:20), you will be safe.

A little genuine grace ensures
The death of all our sins.

Do not waste any time. Do not loiter by the way, for *"the avenger of blood"* is swift of foot; it may be that he is at your heels on this quiet, morning hour.

```
H P S P J D E A X Q W U I Q Q S H Z S C
S T U M B L I N G B L O C K N A N I J S
F P Y V P E B S D W S Y R N E F K S R A
P R E S E N T S A V I O R J O E F X N L
P I C T U R E W T P R O T E C T I O N V
N B O A D F N Z R B B W L O K Y D K E A
W Z C A N A A N E L J D Z V W Y Q Q A T
A E L D E R S F A X U T O E O P U P S I
F V C V O S D N D M O G A R P R A A Y O
J S E T C D I S T A N C E T L E M W P N
U G Q U G F R R W H J E E A A S G E A N
Y I R P Z P E F T F G S U K B E L W S S
U M F S W M K Q I V B Q J E T R S D S T
U B S R O U N D A B O U T N V V P B A R
T J M Q Z Y K Y Q V I I F C W E L J G A
M T B A I N S C R I P T I O N D S P E I
H R E F U G E N Q E Y A V E N G E R Z G
K T W X X Z Q E Z B E N J B O B Z J K H
R E N U N C I A T I O N Z O W E F B T T
H E A V E N T O D B M F N U Y P Q B Z L
```

REFUGE	AVENGER	CANAAN	SALVATION
PRESENT SAVIOR	DISTANCE	RENUNCIATION	PRESERVED
EASY PASSAGE	SAFETY	ELDERS	OVERTAKEN
STUMBLING BLOCK	INSCRIPTION	PICTURE	ROUNDABOUT
STRAIGHT	TREAD	HEAVEN	PROTECTION

DAY 8

Evening

The Father sent the Son to be the Saviour of the world.
—1 John 4:14

It is a sweet thought that Jesus Christ did not come forth without His Father's permission, authority, consent, and assistance. He was sent by the Father so that He might be the Savior of men. We are too apt to forget that, while there are distinctions as to the persons in the Trinity, there are no distinctions of honor. We too frequently ascribe the honor of our salvation, or at least the depths of its benevolence, more to Jesus Christ than to the Father. This is a very great mistake. What if Jesus came? Did not His Father send Him? If He spoke wondrously, did not His Father pour grace into His lips so that He might be an able minister of the new covenant? He who knows the Father, the Son, and the Holy Spirit, as he should know them, never sets one before another in his love. He sees them at Bethlehem, at Gethsemane, and on Calvary, all equally engaged in the work of salvation. O Christian, have you put your confidence in the Man Christ Jesus? Have you placed your reliance solely on Him? Are you united with Him? Then believe that you are united with the God of heaven. Since to the Man Christ Jesus you are brother, and hold closest fellowship, you are linked thereby with God the Eternal, and *"the Ancient of days"* (Dan. 7:9, 13, 22) is your Father and your Friend. Did you ever consider the depth of love that was in the heart of Jehovah, when God the Father equipped His Son for the great enterprise of mercy? If not, make this your day's meditation. The Father sent Him! Contemplate that subject. Think about how Jesus works what the Father wills. In the wounds of the dying Savior, see the love of the great I Am. Let every thought of Jesus also be connected with the Eternal, ever blessed God, for *"it pleased the Lord to bruise him; he hath put him to grief"* (Isa. 53:10).

```
R X G R Z W V R R P D A A N K V K N B V
A S T E Z M O S N Y B R F U S A T M E O
B G W R T U M N P F C S P U J U R I T M
U E Z O O H Q A D B K Q G D N T A N H D
O W N H R N S M S R T A M E R H Q I L I
L J P E Y K E E I S O K K W Z O S S E S
Y F E E V G O W M T I U E X H R H T H T
X D Z N R O D F C A C S S P R I O E E I
Y M K R G M L M S O N C T L X T N R M N
V Z L F F A I E C A V E A A Y Y O S Y C
C L Z E B N G S N O L E L E N W R Q R T
U Y W Q I E U E S C N V N W C C Y B G I
O N Z J T W U L D I E F A A G C E C J O
U C I K Q N O N R H O R I T N D E Y U N
W T U T C P M X B U S N K D I T C Q D M
M R I S E G W S W E E T U H E O L B K F
P L M R N D C A L V A R Y X K N N O L N
G E E Q U I P P E D V H N A E U C Y F L
Z L Q D A K A D S C O N S E N T X E V D
W Y D U K O C O R D B T R I N I T Y S N
```

SWEET	PERMISSION	AUTHORITY	CONSENT
ASSISTANCE	DISTINCTION	TRINITY	HONOR
BENEVOLENCE	WONDROUSLY	MINISTER	NEW COVENANT
BETHLEHEM	GETHSEMANE	CALVARY	ENGAGED
WORK OF SALVATION	CONFIDENCE	UNITED	EQUIPPED

Morning

Pray one for another.
—James 5:16

As an encouragement to offer intercessory prayer cheerfully, remember that such prayer is the sweetest God ever hears, for the prayer of Christ is of this same character. In all the incense that our Great High Priest now puts into the golden censer, there is not a single grain for Himself. His intercession must be the most acceptable of all supplications—and the more our prayer is like Christ's, the sweeter it will be. Thus while petitions for ourselves will be accepted, our pleadings for others, having in them more of the fruits of the Spirit—more love, more faith, more brotherly kindness—will be, through the precious merits of Jesus, the sweetest offering that we can present to God, the very fat of our sacrifice. Remember, also, that intercessory prayer is exceedingly prevalent. What wonders it has brought about! The Word of God teems with its marvelous deeds. Believer, you have a mighty engine in your hand; use it well, and use it constantly. Use it with faith, and you will surely be a benefactor to your brethren. When you have the King's ear, speak to Him for the suffering members of His body. When you are favored to draw very near to His throne, and the King says to you, *"Whatsoever ye shall ask the Father in my name, he will give it you"* (John 16:23), let your petitions be, not for yourself alone, but for the many who need His aid. If you have grace at all and you are not an intercessor, that grace must be as small as a grain of mustard seed. You have just enough grace to float your soul clear from the quicksand, but you have no deep floods of grace. Otherwise, you would carry in your joyous boat a weighty cargo of the needs of others, and you would bring back from your Lord rich blessings, which without you they might not have obtained.

Oh, let my hands forget their skill,
My tongue be silent, cold, and still,
This bounding heart forget to beat,
If I forget the mercy seat!

```
Y N J H I G H P R I E S T R H F R M M O
H W F O H B H E M I P R A Y E R Z K E D
Y M X R O F A K I N D N E S S Y P Q N I
O I K X U H N W I R E Q B M X U Z A C Z
S N I B Z I O R V N M T S E C C P C O X
W F G C Z X T P L A C S V R U F E C U G
E K A E E N H O G O S E U I E Q T E R J
E G W P A A E U F S V I N T X B I P A B
T I S M K R R R C T S E I S L Z T T G C
E A N F T J O C V Q H V G R E V I A E H
S O M L E C C O G T O E E N B I O B M E
T R E M E M B E R Z D F S D J J N L E E
I L A Y Z D W K F A I T H P Z X S E N R
W I N T E R C E S S I O N B I O K V T F
X B D B G K D B Z C U J Y A S R G B L U
X W M R C D Z L O K L E O F V F I H B L
P J Y O K W C Q P K H U K W X L K T O L
N T G O L D E N W Z J C S C E N S E R Y
C H A R A C T E R X F M O N R I U M S V
F P D C O P L E A D I N G S D B B T Z S
```

PRAYER	ANOTHER	ENCOURAGEMENT	INTERCESSION
CHEERFULLY	REMEMBER	SWEETEST	CHARACTER
INCENSE	HIGH PRIEST	GOLDEN	CENSER
ACCEPTABLE	PETITIONS	PLEADINGS	FRUIT OF THE SPIRIT
LOVE	FAITH	KINDNESS	MERITS

Evening

Arise ye, and depart.
—Micah 2:10

The hour is approaching when the message will come to us, as it comes to all—"Arise, and leave the home in which you have dwelled. Leave the city in which you have done your business. Leave your family and friends. Arise, and take your last journey." And what do we know of the journey? What do we know of the country to which we are bound? We have read a little about it, and some has been revealed to us by the Spirit, but how little we know of the realms of the future! We know that there is a black and stormy river called Death. God bids us cross it, promising to be with us. And, after death, what comes? What wondrous world will open to our astonished sight? What scene of glory will be unfolded to our view? No traveler has ever returned to tell. But we know enough of the heavenly land to make us welcome with joy and gladness our summons there. The journey of death may be dark, but we may go forth on it fearlessly, knowing that God is with us as we walk through the gloomy valley; therefore, we need fear no evil. We will be departing from all we have known and loved here, but we will be going to our Father's house—to our Father's home, where Jesus is—to that royal *"city which hath foundations, whose builder and maker is God"* (Heb. 11:10). This will be our last removal, to dwell forever with Him whom we love, in the midst of His people, in the presence of God. Christian, meditate much on heaven. It will help you to press on and to forget the toil of the way. This vale of tears is but the pathway to the better country. This world of woe is but the stepping-stone to a world of bliss.

Prepare us, Lord, by grace divine,
    For Thy bright courts on high;
Then bid our spirits rise,
    And join the chorus of the sky.

```
S G M V S R O G I A I G K U H W B F V R
Y B G R G W I S T X G O V F J W A E C K
O S P I W Y B B G N C I Q E U O X M O A
O U J V M A A P P R O A C H I N G J U Y
J M P E B E E P Z W R D X M B D T O N E
V M U R B P S X R E L A P A Q R Q U T K
A O I N D A H S X V Z S L X F O N R R E
L N H K F O E N A J O T A E H U B N Y H
L S R A Y O A R Z G R O R B S S N E F R
E Q O W V S L Q Y O E N I H P O U Y I E
Y A C N B Y D D V C V I S F R Y N N Q V
D W E L L E D Y E Q R S E D E P A R T E
T L E F F C J N E D A H Y X D F D Z U A
X H W D B U R G N I K E E N S K C R K L
U X F P P B G G M Y E D V K R Y L C O E
C R O S S V F Z S J R E A L M S X J A D
N G F U T U R E G L O R Y V R V X P U B
N V I O N C U E V Z X F P X X U B S V C
Z F E A R L E S S L Y L C V J R I X W W
E H V J V B U S I N E S S O V H Q I E R
```

ARISE YE	DEPART	APPROACHING	MESSAGE
DWELLED	BUSINESS	JOURNEY	COUNTRY
REVEALED	REALMS	FUTURE	RIVER
CROSS	WONDROUS	ASTONISHED	GLORY
UNFOLDED	SUMMONS	FEARLESSLY	VALLEY

Morning

He shall save his people from their sins.
—Matthew 1:21

Many persons, when asked what they mean by salvation, will reply, "Being saved from hell and taken to heaven." This is one result of salvation, but it is not one tenth of what is contained in that blessing. It is true that our Lord Jesus Christ redeems all His people from the wrath to come. He saves them from the fearful condemnation that their sins have brought upon them, but His triumph is far more complete than this. He saves His people *"from their sins."* Oh, sweet deliverance from our worst foes! Where Christ works a saving work, He casts Satan from his throne and will not let him be master any longer. No man is a true Christian if sin reigns in his mortal body. Sin will be in us; it will never be utterly expelled until the spirit enters glory, but it will never have dominion. There will be a striving for dominion—a lusting against the new law and the new spirit that God has implanted—but sin will never get the upper hand so as to be absolute monarch of our natures. Christ will be the Master of the heart, and sin must be mortified. The Lion of the tribe of Judah will prevail, and the dragon will be cast out. Believer, is sin subdued in you? If your life is unholy, your heart is unchanged; and if your heart is unchanged, you are an unsaved person. If the Savior has not sanctified you, renewed you, given you a hatred of sin and a love of holiness, He has done nothing in you of a saving character. Grace that does not make a man better than others is a worthless counterfeit. Christ saves His people, not *in* their sins, but *from* them. Without *"holiness,…no man shall see the Lord"* (Heb. 12:14). *"Let every one that nameth the name of Christ depart from iniquity"* (2 Tim. 2:19). If we are not saved from sin, how will we hope to be counted among His people? Lord, save me now from all evil and enable me to honor my Savior.

```
K A H X K B P B H U L A T O J F D F U D
U B E K D E T L C F Z Y C S G I R L T P
T S W E E P R E V A I L O P S C W G L U
F O V S L Z P S R J S S M B N Z E Y H P
U L Z Y I T V S H B M S P N A W O R U P
B U R G V R T I F T M Q L Z L T S Q Q E
S T K L E S X N L A A Z E N X X A T R R
N E C V R P A G T U S X T Y M N L D S H
U G E E A G W V G G T Q E E T N V O S A
E R L Y N F A R E Q E X X V G O A M G N
W N O H C O K W A D R I F W X G T I T D
H F R L E Y H S D T F R B A L B I N R P
N P K B M O N A R C H R E J E S O I I H
C O N D E M N A T I O N O D C K N O U E
P M L I G W E K L F Z C W M E I L N M A
P B Q T D V T R S C H M I B H E I J P V
E N M M N S P J R E I G N S K E M J H E
C X W O R S T F O E H G J W Q D L S L N
E X P E L L E D R I Q O H P B V R L B Q
I C Q E M O N E W S P I R I T W F C Q B
```

SALVATION	SAVED FROM HELL	HEAVEN	BLESSING
REDEEMS	WRATH	CONDEMNATION	TRIUMPH
COMPLETE	DELIVERANCE	WORST FOE	MASTER
REIGNS	EXPELLED	DOMINION	NEW SPIRIT
UPPER HAND	ABSOLUTE	MONARCH	PREVAIL

I know how to abound.
—Philippians 4:12

Many who know *"how to be abased"* (Phil. 4:12) have not learned *"how to abound."* On top of a pinnacle, their heads grow dizzy, and they are ready to fall. The Christian more often disgraces his profession of faith in prosperity than in adversity. It is a dangerous thing to be prosperous. The crucible of adversity is a less severe trial to the Christian than the refinery of prosperity. Oh, what leanness of soul and neglect of spiritual things have been brought on through the very mercies and bounties of God! Yet this does not need to happen, for the apostle Paul said that he knew how to abound. When he had much, he knew how to use it. Abundant grace enabled him to bear abundant prosperity. When he had a full sail, he was loaded with much ballast and so floated safely. More than human skill is needed to carry an overflowing cup of mortal joy with a steady hand, yet Paul had learned that skill, for he declared, *"In all things I am instructed both to be full and to be hungry"* (Phil. 4:12). It is a divine lesson to know how to be full, for the Israelites were full once, but while the meat was yet in their mouths, the wrath of God came on them. Many have asked for mercies so that they might satisfy their own hearts' lusts. When we have much of God's providential mercies, it often happens that we have but little of God's grace and little gratitude for the bounties we have received. We are full and we forget God. Satisfied with earth, we are content to do without heaven. Rest assured that it is harder to know how to be full than it is to know how to be hungry, so desperate is the tendency of human nature to pride and forgetfulness of God. Take care that you ask in your prayers that God would teach you how to be full.

Let not the gifts Thy love bestows
　　Estrange our hearts from Thee.

```
K A C N O V E R F L O W I N G E K U J P
X T W I B S X X S T E A D Y H A N D M I
S M Q S A W G W V E T B U H L T G B W N
G C P R O F E S S I O N O V S J R I I N
E R A B A L L A S T A R U S D Z A J H A
N U Z B Y W G A B O U N D X B K T B N C
G C I N K Q D Z B B F H K B O S I J E L
M I B M D R E F I N E R Y S U D T A G E
C B E Y W B L C G A V C J A N F U P L T
Q L S U G V M I F W H L V D T G D Q E D
F E T X P H A B U I Y I J E I E E Y C W
Z C O E K A D V E R S I T Y E E U A T P
I G W I K U F J E C C A S Q S B K B R A
X I S E M A O D K L P C O G R Z K U A M
Q F K T C N Q H J E M T A B D R E N H I
L E A N N E S S D A G D I Z Z Y B D X W
H U M A N S K I L L I O M Y Z O R A N C
Y U B P R O S P E R I T Y U J I O N K V
Y O D E Q Z Y L E P E L Y R U Q Q T E B
M O R T A L J O Y S E M E R C I E S T V
```

ABOUND	PINNACLE	DIZZY	PROFESSION
PROSPERITY	ADVERSITY	CRUCIBLE	REFINERY
LEANNESS	NEGLECT	MERCIES	BOUNTIES
ABUNDANT	BALLAST	OVERFLOWING	MORTAL JOY
STEADY HAND	HUMAN SKILL	BESTOWS	GRATITUDE

Morning

I have blotted out, as a thick cloud, thy transgressions, and, as a cloud, thy sins: return unto me; for I have redeemed thee.
—Isaiah 44:22

Carefully observe the instructive comparison made here: our sins are like a cloud. As clouds are of many shapes and shades, so are our transgressions. As clouds obscure the light of the sun and darken the landscape below, so do our sins hide from us the light of Jehovah's face and cause us to sit in the shadow of death. They are earthborn things and rise from the miry places of our nature. When so collected that their measure is full, they threaten us with storm and tempest. Sadly, unlike clouds, our sins do not yield any beneficial showers; rather, they threaten to deluge us with a fiery flood of destruction. O black clouds of sin, how can it be fair weather with our souls while you remain? Let our joyful eyes dwell on the notable act of divine mercy—blotting out. God Himself appears on the scene, and in divine graciousness, instead of manifesting His anger, He reveals His grace. At once and forever, He effectively removes the mischief, not by blowing away the cloud, but by blotting it out from existence once and for all. No sin remains against the justified man; the great transaction of the Cross has eternally removed his transgressions from him. On Calvary's summit the great deed, by which the sin of all the chosen was forever put away, was completely and effectively performed. Practically, let us obey the gracious command, *"Return unto me."* Why should pardoned sinners live at a distance from their God? If we have been forgiven of all our sins, let no fear keep us from the boldest access to our Lord. Let us regret any backslidings, but let us not persevere in them. To the greatest possible nearness of communion with the Lord, let us, in the power of the Holy Spirit, strive mightily to return. O Lord, this night restore us!

A P X N K S U G J E H O V A H G T P Y L
V L C P O Q L M A N I F E S T I N G J J
Z R A J P T N L C O M P A R I S O N S D
A E G N G M A U L L S I O W V U N R Z E
I T E O D Y Z B W L O F M E U V Q E V X
N U B E B S U K L O C Z Z E R L K G N I
S R B Q Y S C O P E H K V I U G W W P S
T N L B T H C A E F F E C T I V E L Y T
R A U L R H Q U P D W B K Z D L E N T E
U F K R I J L P R E C O V B B O H X I N
C P L J X O R J W E H H H Y F I Y D E C
T C U B U P H T H I C K C L O U D S A E
I R A C O Y T R A N S A C T I O N H R S
V S M Y R E D E E M E D V D V X V A T E
E D I V I N E M E R C Y T U T K S P H H
E R I G W M L O C G Q E G Z L B Z E B X
H V T R A N S G R E S S I O N S D S O C
G K U J U S T I F I E D R S J F D I R R
S H A D E S Q B L O T T E D O U T H N I
H B U D I F C W I V U Q W Z V C B X E J

BLOTTED OUT	THICK CLOUD	TRANSGRESSIONS	RETURN
REDEEMED	INSTRUCTIVE	COMPARISON	SHAPES
SHADES	OBSCURE	LANDSCAPE	JEHOVAH
EARTHBORN	NOTABLE	DIVINE MERCY	MANIFESTING
EXISTENCE	JUSTIFIED	TRANSACTION	EFFECTIVELY

Evening

Behold, what manner of love the Father hath bestowed upon us, that we should be called the sons of God: therefore the world knoweth us not, because it knew him not. Beloved, now are we the sons of God.
—1 John 3:1–2

"*Behold, what manner of love the Father hath bestowed upon us.*" Consider who we were, and what we feel ourselves to be even now when corruption is powerful in us, and you will wonder at our adoption. Yet we are called "*the sons of God.*" What a significant relationship is that of a son, and what privileges it brings! What care and tenderness the son expects from his father, and what love the father feels toward the son! But all that, and more than that, we now have through Christ. As for the temporary drawback of suffering with the Elder Brother, this we accept as an honor: "*Therefore the world knoweth us not, because it knew him not.*" We are content to be unknown with Him in His humiliation, for we are to be exalted with Him. "*Beloved, now are we the sons of God.*" That is easy to read, but it is not so easy to feel. How is it with your heart this morning? Are you in the lowest depths of sorrow? Does corruption rise within your spirit and grace seem like a poor spark trampled underfoot? Does your faith almost fail you? Fear not! It is neither your graces nor your feelings on which you are to live: you must live simply by faith on Christ. With all these things against us, "*now*"—in the very depths of our sorrow, wherever we may be—"*now,*" as much in the valley as on the mountain, "*Beloved, now are we the sons of God.*" "Ah, but," you say, "see how I am clothed! My graces are not bright; my righteousness does not shine with apparent glory." But read the next part: "*It doth not yet appear what we shall be: but we know that, when he shall appear, we shall be like him*" (1 John 3:2). The Holy Spirit will purify our minds, and divine power will refine our bodies; then we will "*see him as he is*" (v. 2).

```
S T V A D O P T I O N K Q F J W S A H N
C X W A J H R F I J R G S E K Q I V Z H
T M A N N E R O F L O V E E M G G X Z X
T D A T H B I Y B Q H G J L J P N B H V
T E D H W M O U N T A I N I B U I E E A
E W M F F G O V E D Z U T N R S F S L L
N I J P H O P H I W R I A G I H I T T L
D I K K O E K C J B E A A S G B C O T E
E K P P O R J J L V Q I W A H G A W N Y
R Y L Z S D A U T G I W E B T Y N E B S
N E L D E R B R O T H E R V A C T D W O
E M P Q L X O N Y U D A N W L C D S C N
S C P N X Z S S E B W T C S U O K V E G
S G R N G O B E H O L D Z Z A U G B X S
H U M I L I A T I O N I W O N D E R A O
R N R R U P S P R I V I L E G E K R L F
A C N J Y C F B F Y Y D S T G Z V S T G
C O R R U P T I O N S T W K V G I F E O
V S B E L O V E D O S G T D O O X J D D
Y Q X H I O W A R E R N Q I S Y S C K B
```

BEHOLD	MANNER OF LOVE	BESTOWED	SONS OF GOD
BELOVED	CORRUPTION	WONDER	ADOPTION
SIGNIFICANT	PRIVILEGE	TENDERNESS	TEMPORARY
DRAWBACK	ELDER BROTHER	HUMILIATION	EXALTED
FEELINGS	BRIGHT	VALLEY	MOUNTAIN

Morning

There is therefore now no condemnation.
—Romans 8:1

Come, my soul, think of this: By believing in Jesus, you are actually and effectively cleared from guilt. You are released from your prison. No longer chained like a slave, you are delivered from the bondage of the law. You are freed from sin and can walk as a freeman. Your Savior's blood has obtained your full pardon. Now, you have the right to approach your Father's throne. No flames of vengeance and no fiery swords are there to scare you. Justice cannot smite the innocent. Your disabilities are taken away. You were once unable to see your Father's face; you can see it now. You could not speak with Him, but now you have access with boldness. Once the fear of hell was upon you. But you have no fear of it now, for how can there be punishment for the guiltless? He who believes is not condemned and cannot be punished. And more than all, the privileges you might have enjoyed, if you had never sinned, are yours now that you are justified. All the blessings that you would have had if you had kept the law, and more, are yours, because Christ has kept it for you. All the love and the acceptance that perfect obedience could have obtained from God belong to you, because Christ was perfectly obedient on your behalf. He has imputed all His merits to your account so that you might be exceedingly rich through Him, who for your sake became exceedingly poor. Oh, how great the debt of love and gratitude you owe to your Savior!

A debtor to mercy alone,
  Of covenant mercy I sing;
Nor fear with Your righteousness on,
  My person and offerings to bring:
The terrors of law and of God,
  With me can have nothing to do;
My Savior's obedience and blood
  Hide all my transgressions from view.

```
C L E A R E D X Z A N S B E L H V A E Y
P Y D P K S N E N C H A I N E D D X A R
Q H W U R X T R N C W I N N O C E N T O
Y M P U N I S H M E N T I P P H P U P I
R A F T V W S X O P O Z K P E T N H E G
D E P F X Y W O X T U V E P P N A U R D
X D L P P B E E N A P Y P O B M C M F B
X D Q E R M M V D N G Y Z G Z G C C E Z
A B X E A O I D W C R U Q Q F B E X C O
W F Z B U S A R S E J Q I A K O S E T K
R B U R W F E C H A R Y C L G L S V O B
V I M P U T E D H V P L H G T D W O B O
A E K W R X Q B F R E E M A N N C L D N
P L A X P B E L U D C D F O N E T T I D
T C Y C M D E L I V E R E D T S T B E A
B E L I E V I N G F R S F M A S L T N G
G U I L T L E S S K S H W L K O M O C E
A Z R A E Z J K Z V P H U R F D T C E V
C R B M L Z Q S M W M E R I T S T L V O
N O C O N D E M N A T I O N T X O F U Q
```

NO CONDEMNATION	BELIEVING	CLEARED	GUILT
RELEASED	PRISON	CHAINED	BONDAGE
DELIVERED	FREE MAN	APPROACH	INNOCENT
ACCESS	BOLDNESS	PUNISHMENT	GUILTLESS
ACCEPTANCE	PERFECT OBEDIENCE	IMPUTED	MERITS

Evening

I have learned, in whatsoever state I am, therewith to be content.
—Philippians 4:11

These words show us that contentment is not a natural human inclination. Covetousness, discontentment, and complaining are as natural to man as weeds are to the soil. We need not sow thistles and brambles; they come up naturally enough, because they are indigenous to earth. Similarly, we do not need to teach men to complain; they complain fast enough without any education. But the precious things of the earth must be cultivated. If we would have wheat, we must plough and sow. If we want flowers, we must plant and care for a garden. Now, contentment is one of the flowers of heaven, and if we would have it, it must be cultivated. It will not grow in us by nature. It is the new nature alone that can produce it, and even then we must be especially careful and watchful that we maintain and cultivate the grace that God has sown in us. Paul said, *"I have learned…to be content."* This statement implies that he did not know how to be content at one time. It cost him some pains to arrive at the mystery of that great truth. No doubt he sometimes thought he had learned the lesson, and then broke down. And when at last he had attained it, and could say, *"I have learned, in whatsoever state I am, therewith to be content,"* he was an old gray-headed man, on the borders of the grave—a poor prisoner shut up in Nero's dungeon in Rome. We might well be willing to endure Paul's infirmities and share the cold dungeon with him, if we, too, might by any means attain his good position. Do not indulge the notion that you can be contented with learning, or learn without discipline. It is not a power that may be exercised naturally, but a science to be acquired gradually. We know this from experience. Brother, hush that grumbling, natural though it be, and continue to be a diligent pupil in the College of Contentment.

```
F T H I S T L E S L N D P Y T O K F C B
D F B V T V T C B C O N T E N T E H O R
D U N G E O N T U P P M S U K E O B V A
L I W W V H A L B L C O L L E G E H E M
D G C H R T Z S P C T D T U J I V E T B
D C W G H C O M P L A I N I N G F T O L
G V J R S W W U A E N L V F I O U E U E
M R C E Q L B R G X O I I A C M L P S S
Y C E D Q N C F D S B G N W T Y H R N B
S N E A Q E H T Z M G E C M K E P E E X
T W H A T S O E V E R N L A X Z D C S F
E P I Q X T E A K W V T I T L K M I S L
R H L K W H R H J M O U N T J P P O Z O
Y A D E V T U U S U G K A A O I R U F W
M T K Z S L Y K T T G R T I Q F O S P E
H H J J T S H H O H Q T I N K G D K Z R
J T E S S Z O B A Z T H O E N R U H L Z
M Y A U H B X N J L R H N D K I C G G W
P L O U G H H X Q S B N Z K V D E O N I
J T M A I N T A I N T Z D H R Y I C T I
```

WHATSOEVER	CONTENT	INCLINATION	COVETOUSNESS
COMPLAINING	THISTLES	BRAMBLES	PRECIOUS
CULTIVATED	PLOUGH	PRODUCE	FLOWER
MAINTAIN	MYSTERY	GREAT TRUTH	LESSON
ATTAINED	DUNGEON	COLLEGE	DILIGENT

Morning

Thy good spirit.
—Nehemiah 9:20

Common, too common, is the sin of forgetting the Holy Spirit. This is folly and ingratitude. He deserves our best, for He is good, supremely good. As God, He is good essentially. He shares in the threefold ascription of *"Holy, holy, holy"* (Isa. 6:3; Rev. 4:8), which ascends to the triune Jehovah. He is purity, truth, and grace. He is good benevolently, tenderly bearing with our waywardness and striving with our rebellious wills. He quickens us from our death in sin, and then He trains us for the skies as a loving nurse fosters her child. How generous, forgiving, and tender is this patient Spirit of God! He is good operatively. All His works are good in the most eminent degree. He suggests good thoughts, prompts good actions, reveals good truths, applies good promises, assists in good attainments, and leads to good results. There is no spiritual good in all the world of which He is not the author and sustainer; heaven itself will owe the perfect character of its redeemed inhabitants to His work. He is good officially. Whether as Comforter, Instructor, Guide, Sanctifier, Quickener, or Intercessor, He fulfills His office well, and each work is laden with the highest good to the church of God. Those who yield to His influences become good, those who obey His impulses do good, and those who live under His power receive good. Let us then act toward so good a person according to the dictates of gratitude. Let us revere and adore Him, *"who is over all, God blessed for ever"* (Rom. 9:5). Let us recognize His power and admit our need of Him by waiting on Him in all our holy enterprises. Let us hourly seek His aid and never grieve Him. And let us praise Him whenever any opportunity to do so arises. The church will never prosper until more reverently it believes in the Holy Spirit. He is so good and kind that it is sad indeed that He should be grieved by slights and neglect.

```
W  S  A  H  F  H  X  K  Z  Q  F  G  C  Y  X  A  E  R  F  K
E  U  Q  R  T  H  R  E  E  F  O  L  D  M  U  O  D  F  O  W
Q  P  P  D  T  N  G  Q  Q  O  E  A  L  E  S  P  G  Y  R  A
I  R  G  K  Z  U  P  H  K  F  O  U  B  O  D  E  A  R  G  Y
B  E  R  R  Q  A  U  A  D  N  V  L  N  L  P  R  R  M  E  W
Z  M  A  F  Z  S  R  P  O  C  Z  W  P  C  G  A  L  K  T  A
R  E  C  J  Z  C  I  P  D  M  H  G  T  M  B  T  F  M  T  R
C  L  E  J  A  R  T  Q  X  U  D  Z  E  X  E  I  F  T  I  D
F  Y  C  H  P  I  Y  O  N  T  L  E  N  X  N  V  S  R  N  N
T  G  K  R  P  P  Q  S  S  R  N  P  D  C  E  E  K  U  G  E
E  O  H  T  L  T  O  W  B  I  H  V  E  C  V  L  N  T  O  S
N  O  N  X  I  I  E  E  U  U  R  S  R  P  O  Y  I  H  Y  S
V  D  R  D  E  O  Y  Z  R  N  O  W  F  O  L  L  Y  Y  W  B
A  C  V  V  S  N  W  M  H  E  S  E  Y  O  E  M  E  Z  J  W
X  G  O  O  D  S  P  I  R  I  T  K  E  O  N  P  G  E  J  U
F  O  R  G  I  V  I  N  G  T  J  S  O  L  T  Q  Y  L  C  Z
I  Q  N  V  J  B  N  T  L  P  A  T  I  E  N  T  Y  C  Y  M
M  V  G  E  N  E  R  O  U  S  E  Y  U  T  D  A  Y  H  Q  M
Q  U  Z  R  A  D  C  P  Y  R  L  A  S  S  I  S  T  S  V  I
X  I  I  N  G  R  A  T  I  T  U  D  E  C  U  N  P  R  O  B
```

GOOD SPIRIT	FORGETTING	FOLLY	INGRATITUDE
SUPREMELY GOOD	THREEFOLD	ASCRIPTION	TRIUNE
PURITY	TRUTH	GRACE	BENEVOLENT
WAYWARDNESS	GENEROUS	FORGIVING	TENDER
PATIENT	OPERATIVELY	ASSISTS	APPLIES

Evening

Show me wherefore thou contendest with me.
—Job 10:2

Perhaps, O tried soul, the Lord is doing this to develop your graces. Some of your graces would never be discovered if it were not for your trials. Do you not know that your faith never looks so grand in summer weather as it does in winter? Love is too often like a glowworm, showing but little light unless it is in the midst of surrounding darkness. Hope itself is like a star—not to be seen in the sunshine of prosperity and only to be discovered in the night of adversity. Afflictions are often the black foils in which God sets the jewels of His children's graces, to make them shine the better. It was but a little while ago that on your knees you were saying, "Lord, I fear I have no faith. Let me know that I have faith." Were you not really, though perhaps unconsciously, praying for trials—for how can you know that you have faith until your faith is exercised? Depend on it: God often sends us trials so that our graces may be discovered, and so that we may be certified of their existence. Besides, it is not merely discovery. Real growth in grace is the result of sanctified trials. God often takes away our comforts and our privileges in order to make us better Christians. He trains His soldiers not in tents of ease and luxury, but by turning them out and sending them on forced marches and into hard service. He makes them ford through streams, swim through rivers, climb mountains, and walk many long miles with heavy knapsacks of sorrow on their backs. Well, Christian, may not this account for the troubles through which you are passing? Is not the Lord bringing out your graces and making them grow? Is this not the reason that He is contending with you?

> Trials make the promise sweet;
> Trials give new life to prayer;
> Trials bring me to His feet,
> Lay me low, and keep me there.

```
O N Y O Q G T S A Z W X S I F Z K L Y D
W S O P Q R L N X K G I U T M K E V J E
T C G T M C M H G K G N N D S N X Y X V
C K O G K T R A I N S F S T C T E R K E
C E N N Y V P Z S V U S H A E H R R K L
N V R A T L J C N O A E I Q B R C I D O
J R C T P E L L L D L G N F O A I T S P
R A S A I S N O W B Y D E E R F S V C S
W S U T T F A D Y C Z U I D C S E Z G O
Z N M B R G I C I W E P P E K W D L R E
X P M X O Q M E K N H K I Q R F E O O P
A O E V U F G T D S G M E I M S Y X W E
J M R G B V D I S C O V E R E D W F I E
R S M R L J B R P A S S I N G I E A N E
Z Y G W E X G R A N D M Q G E L A S G W
P P P L S I G D H R E R X E D I T I R B
E X I S T E N C E G Q G Q U M P H D A B
B F D F H M M H R Y M D F J G N E E C S
V H S E R V I C E S J E W E L S R M E D
X E G L O W W O R M L U E J T D G Q K D
```

DEVELOP	DISCOVERED	GRAND	SUMMER
WEATHER	WINTER	GLOWWORM	SUNSHINE
JEWELS	EXERCISED	CERTIFIED	EXISTENCE
TRAINS	SOLDIERS	SERVICE	KNAPSACKS
TROUBLES	PASSING	CONTENDING	GROW IN GRACE

Morning

Father, I have sinned.
—Luke 15:18

It is quite certain that those whom Christ has washed in His precious blood do not need to make a confession of sin as culprits or criminals before God the Judge. Christ has forever taken away all their sins in a legal sense, so that they no longer stand where they can be condemned, but they are once and for all *"accepted in the beloved"* (Eph. 1:6). But having become children, and offending as children, should they not every day go before their heavenly Father and confess their sin and acknowledge their iniquity in that character? Nature teaches that it is the duty of erring children to make a confession to their earthly father, and the grace of God in the heart teaches us that we, as Christians, owe the same duty to our heavenly Father. We daily offend and should not rest without daily pardon. Suppose that my trespasses against my Father are not at once taken to Him to be washed away by the cleansing power of the Lord Jesus; what will be the consequence? If I have not sought forgiveness and been cleansed from these offenses against my Father, I will feel at a distance from Him. I will doubt His love for me. I will tremble in His presence, and I will be afraid to pray to Him. I will become like the Prodigal, who, although he was his father's child, was still far away from his father. But if, with a child's sorrow at offending so gracious and loving a Parent, I go to Him and tell Him all, and I do not rest until I realize that I am forgiven, then I will feel a holy love toward my Father. I will go through my Christian life not only as saved, but also as one enjoying present peace in God through Jesus Christ my Lord. There is a wide distinction between confessing sin as a culprit and confessing sin as a child. The Father's heart is the place for penitent confessions. We have been cleansed once and for all, but, as children of God, our feet still need to be washed from the defilement of our daily walk.

```
P C I L Y F W T C W A S H E D V B A Y K
R G T I F N B U L P X R F G A P P D Y Z
E A C K N O W L E D G E W V Z D R G W A
S K V O H S H J A H F J Z G T V E O L D
E C E Z V G V G N E F E F H K T C D Q G
N L L I N I Q U I T Y D C O O C I T C I
T E X L C Q Z R N C S O U G H T O H P C
P A R Y R A R M G N U H L Y G E U E R U
E N K W I U W N P E F N B E A G S J O L
A S T X M W C Y O S R K T S C D B U D P
C E V U I K I I W S T S Z S C H L D I R
E D D K N K D F E F M K L P E W O G G I
P R N G A B T N R P W B S Q P W O E A T
D E C Q L T B E Y J Z E R R T S D L L S
S S O L S R E L P A R E N T E I X E O T
D A I L Y P A R D O N P S K D J H G D D
N T R E S P A S S E S U R F H D E A T O
U B X X A U H O L Y L O V E C V K L I Z
I C H R I S T I A N L I F E P T S M E T
B F L V K R A F O R G I V E N E S S N C
```

WASHED	PRECIOUS BLOOD	CULPRITS	CRIMINALS
GOD THE JUDGE	LEGAL	ACCEPTED	ACKNOWLEDGE
INIQUITY	DAILY PARDON	TRESPASSES	CLEANING POWER
SOUGHT	FORGIVENESS	CLEANSED	PRODIGAL
PARENT	HOLY LOVE	CHRISTIAN LIFE	PRESENT PEACE

Evening

[Andrew] first findeth his own brother Simon.
—John 1:41

This case is an excellent example of what happens when spiritual life is vital. As soon as a man has found Christ, he begins to find others. I will not believe that you have tasted of the honey of the Gospel if you can eat it all yourself. True grace puts an end to all spiritual monopoly. Andrew first found his own brother Simon and then others. Relationship has a very strong demand upon our initial individual efforts. Andrew did well to begin with Simon. I do not doubt that there are some Christians giving away tracts at other people's houses who would do well to give away a tract at their own. Likewise, I wonder whether there are not some who are engaged in works of ministry abroad who are neglecting their special sphere of usefulness at home. You may or may not be called to evangelize people in a particular locality, but certainly you are called to see after your own household, your own relatives, and your acquaintances. Let your religion begin at home. Many tradesmen export their best commodities—the Christian should not. All his conversation everywhere should carry the best aroma; but let him pay special care to put forth the sweetest fruit of spiritual life and testimony among his own family. When Andrew went to find his brother, he could not have imagined how eminent Simon would become. Simon Peter was worth ten Andrews as far as we can gather from sacred history, yet Andrew was instrumental in bringing him to Jesus. You may be very deficient in talent yourself, yet you may be the means of drawing to Christ one who will become prominent in grace and service. Dear friend, little do you know the possibilities that are in you. You may merely speak a word to a child, and in that child there may be slumbering a noble heart that will stir the Christian church in years to come. Andrew had only two talents, but he found Peter. Go and do likewise.

```
R P M C C R E I T D C M X D U K C M E I
E W G F W D M Z R Y O Y Y Z S B P K A Y
L E M B N C D J A B M F U H E F I N C H
A J U O Z R B H C F M R S Z F U L T Q M
T Y S C N P E A T Q O V E D U Y J F U P
I X I D D O N L S Z D I M T L I H W A L
O I N Y Z C P R A L I T V C N N O D I D
N P D F Y C S O W T T A A V E I U A N E
S F I D C F S U L N I L Y Z S T S T T N
H O V X I K E I V Y E V E R S I E N A U
I M I R T V A L M U S I E S G A H N N J
P S D T T H U U B O F P C S J L O U C V
D Z U E W P N K Y X N I M V A O L F E O
Q D A A A O N I Y B U Y I B B P D Z S R
B G L U N B Q A N E V A N G E L I Z E N
K Y L N D E L L K Q E F F O R T S D J E
R C V Z R S P I R I T U A L L I F E C W
W A W M E J Z F I N D O T H E R S W U Q
A B O W W M I N I S T R Y Y O L F P O J
J Q L L O C A L I T Y H O N E Y A V B J
```

ANDREW	SIMON	SPIRITUAL LIFE	VITAL
FIND OTHERS	HONEY	MONOPOLY	RELATIONSHIP
INITIAL	INDIVIDUAL	EFFORTS	TRACTS
MINISTRY	USEFULNESS	EVANGELIZE	LOCALITY
HOUSEHOLD	RELATIVES	ACQUAINTANCES	COMMODITIES

Morning

His bow abode in strength, and the arms of his hands were made strong by the hands of the mighty God of Jacob.
—Genesis 49:24

The strength that God gives to His Josephs is real strength. It is not a boasted valor; fiction; or a thing of which men talk, but that ends in smoke; it is true, divine strength. How did Joseph stand against temptation? Because God gave him aid. There is nothing that we can do without the power of God. All true strength comes from *"the mighty God of Jacob."* Notice in what a blessedly familiar way God gives this strength to Joseph: *"The arms of his hands were made strong by the hands of the mighty God of Jacob."* Thus God is represented as putting His hands on Joseph's hands, placing His arms on Joseph's arms. As a father teaches his children, so the Lord teaches them who fear Him. He puts His arms on them. Marvelous condescension! God Almighty, eternal, omnipotent, stoops from His throne and lays His hands on the child's hand, stretching His arm on the arm of Joseph so that he may be made strong! This strength was also covenant strength, for it is ascribed to *"the mighty God of Jacob."* Now, wherever you read of the God of Jacob in the Bible, you should remember the covenant with Jacob. Christians love to think of God's covenant. All the power, all the grace, all the blessings, all the mercies, all the comforts, and all the things we have flow to us from the Source, through the covenant. If there were no covenant, then we would fail indeed; for all grace proceeds from it, as light and heat proceed from the sun. No angels ascend or descend, save on that ladder that Jacob saw, at the top of which stood a covenant God. Christian, it may be that the archers have sorely grieved you, shot at you, and wounded you, but still your bow abides in strength; be sure, then, to ascribe all the glory to Jacob's God.

```
B V T H D D F A N W B B P V V G Z B I I
C O N D E S C E N S I O N M W O J L D K
C R E I O M N I P O T E N T Z D Q E O P
D L U B B F F S T R E N G T H O Q S N O
X A S C O M F O R T T E X H R F T S N W
J S J D D E V K V O A Z A B G J C I G E
I C I R R E P R E S E N T E D A O N K R
S R A U J Y M J R K T P Y G J C V G F O
T I Q A K C I R Y T K R D N I O E S J F
R B L X D T Y Y A B I D E U D B N J O G
E E N W I M T K N A M E Y Z Q J A C S O
T D P E O U M Y E C C J O N T F N P E D
C E G C Y G A I S T O O P S J V T X P Z
H N P V A F F E Y N L A C G C V A O H M
I Q Q X I B O A S T E D V A L O R M B B
N H A N D S O F T H E M I G H T Y V H M
G B T P A T E M P T A T I O N Z A D G D
T N Q N G C F B M F T K U Z M U Q J C W
M E R C Y H T X W Y F H B P T N K C G M
Q J L M A R V E L O U S E T E R N A L F
```

ABIDE	STRENGTH	HANDS OF THE MIGHTY	GOD OF JACOB
JOSEPH	BOASTED VALOR	TEMPTATION	POWER OF GOD
REPRESENTED	MARVELOUS	CONDESCENSION	ETERNAL
OMNIPOTENT	STOOPS	STRETCHING	ASCRIBED
COVENANT	BLESSINGS	MERCY	COMFORT

Evening

The LORD is slow to anger, and great in power.
—Nahum 1:3

Jehovah *"is slow to anger."* When mercy comes into the world, it drives winged steeds; the axles of its chariot wheels are red-hot with speed. But when wrath goes forth, it toils on with sluggish footsteps, for God takes no pleasure in the sinner's death. God's rod of mercy is always in His outstretched hands. His sword of justice is in its sheath, held down by the pierced hand of love that bled for the sins of men. *"The LORD is slow to anger"* because He is great in power. He is truly great in power who has power over himself. When God's power restrains Himself, then it is power indeed: the power that binds omnipotence surpasses omnipotence. A man who has a strong mind can bear to be insulted for a long time, and he resents the wrong only when a sense of right demands his action. The weak mind is irritated by little things, but the strong mind bears irritation like a rock that does not move, even though a thousand breakers dash upon it and cast their pitiful malice in spray upon its summit. God sees His enemies, yet He does not rouse Himself to action, but holds in His anger. If He were less divine than He is, long before this, He would have sent forth the whole of His thunders and emptied the magazines of heaven. Long before this, He would have blasted the earth with the wondrous fires of its lower regions, and man would have been utterly destroyed. But the greatness of His power brings us mercy. Dear reader, what is your state of mind this evening? Can you by humble faith look to Jesus and say, "My Substitute, You are my rock and my trust"? Then, beloved, do not be afraid of God's power. If by faith you have fled to Christ for refuge, the power of God no longer needs to terrify you any more than the shield and sword of the warrior terrifies those whom he loves. Instead, rejoice that He who is *"great in power"* is your Father and Friend.

```
Z S I M K N Y R Q D A D D A F M N Z P H
O Z Z R B T F Z B G Q X L E D A I M H A
B B S O Z Y S G R H B Q L J G G Z C C N
A H E D X T B F E K S L T E O A H O R D
Q Z T O F O D O A C L R T P S Z X I G O
C U X F J F U O K U U C E K Z I C U P F
S H S M H W W T E L G G Y T Z N Z Z R L
L P A E R M X S R N G G Z G D E R T H O
O M H R N L P T S O I F E G T S W H L V
W S I C I S S E F M S K G E J W U U Z E
T U R Y I O K P A G H S L A G B F N H W
O B R Y L K T S Q O B Z C W I G P D S H
A S I X G P C V Q I X E U K L M Z E H E
N T T A C P I E R C E D Q X K M G R E E
G I A S W O R D O F J U S T I C E S A L
E T T D W M G R E A T I N P O W E R T S
R U I B F E X R E F U G E B R V Q Y H P
P T O B Y B R Y E I W O J C P X Z T Z R
K E N J D A L J U R E S T R A I N S Q T
C E V Z C P S W I N G E D S T E E D S R
```

SLOW TO ANGER	GREAT IN POWER	WINGED STEEDS	AXLES
CHARIOT	WHEELS	SLUGGISH	FOOTSTEPS
ROD OF MERCY	SWORD OF JUSTICE	SHEATH	PIERCED
HAND OF LOVE	RESTRAINS	IRRITATION	BREAKERS
THUNDERS	MAGAZINES	SUBSTITUTE	REFUGE

Morning

Behold, if the leprosy have covered all his flesh,
he shall pronounce him clean that hath the plague.
—Leviticus 13:13

Although this regulation appears to be strange, there was wisdom in it. The outward manifestation of the disease proved that the leper's constitution was sound. It may be well for us to see the symbolic meaning of so unusual a rule. We, too, are lepers and may apply the law of the leper to ourselves. When a man sees himself to be altogether lost and ruined, covered with the defilement of sin, and in no part free from pollution; when he disclaims all righteousness of his own and pleads guilty before the Lord, then he is clean through the blood of Jesus and the grace of God. Hidden, unfelt, unconfessed iniquity is the true leprosy; but when sin is seen and felt, it has received its deathblow, and the Lord looks with eyes of mercy on the afflicted soul. Nothing is more deadly than self-righteousness or more hopeful than repentance. We must confess that we are sinful, for no confession short of this will be the whole truth. If the Holy Spirit is at work in us, convicting us of sin, there will be no difficulty about making such an acknowledgment—it will spring spontaneously from our lips. What comfort the text gives to truly awakened sinners: the very circumstance that so grievously discouraged them is here turned into a sign of a hopeful condition! Stripping comes before clothing; digging out the foundation is the first thing in building—and a thorough sense of sin is one of the earliest works of grace. Poor, leprous sinner, take heart from the text, and come as you are to Jesus.

For let our debts be what they may,
    However great or small,
As soon as we have nought to pay,
    Our Lord forgives us all.
'Tis perfect poverty alone
    That sets the soul at large:
While we can call one mite our own,
    We have no full discharge.

```
U  C  G  B  Q  W  O  E  P  O  L  L  U  T  I  O  N  H  C  V
C  N  A  D  E  F  I  L  E  M  E  N  T  O  F  S  I  N  P  V
F  E  F  E  Z  Z  C  O  N  S  T  I  T  U  T  I  O  N  M  F
G  Y  X  E  U  N  C  O  N  F  E  S  S  E  D  L  J  B  O  S
O  E  B  C  L  H  I  D  D  E  N  A  V  J  B  M  L  B  E  V
P  U  A  N  L  T  M  S  P  I  C  G  M  T  Q  W  E  D  M  C
K  F  Y  S  I  E  M  X  Z  N  N  A  E  J  V  R  P  W  A  L
G  W  O  S  H  E  A  O  Q  B  I  K  J  Y  K  T  R  G  N  O
M  U  J  U  Y  Z  Q  N  V  B  Z  W  Z  U  I  Q  O  C  I  T
L  D  F  W  H  O  L  E  T  R  U  T  H  N  D  T  S  O  F  H
S  I  Y  A  U  G  V  W  E  W  I  S  D  O  M  C  Y  M  E  I
P  Z  P  E  Z  J  R  E  G  U  L  A  T  I  O  N  D  F  S  N
L  O  S  T  A  N  D  R  U  I  N  E  D  K  V  O  T  O  T  G
U  P  R  O  N  O  U  N  C  E  D  C  L  E  A  N  C  R  A  A
L  G  X  D  V  V  H  U  J  O  O  C  M  Y  W  P  A  T  T  W
W  I  U  K  M  J  X  Y  M  P  R  A  H  C  U  Y  O  R  I  B
Y  F  B  P  E  K  A  D  S  Y  M  B  O  L  I  C  R  S  O  Y
P  B  F  O  U  N  D  A  T  I  O  N  F  B  I  N  K  K  N  Z
O  K  A  C  K  N  O  W  L  E  G  E  M  E  N  T  K  M  W  I
T  L  C  R  S  K  R  I  G  H  T  E  O  U  S  N  E  S  S  I
```

LEPROSY	PRONOUNCED CLEAN	REGULATION	WISDOM
MANIFESTATION	CONSTITUTION	SYMBOLIC	LOST AND RUINED
DEFILEMENT OF SIN	POLLUTION	RIGHTEOUSNESS	CLEAN
HIDDEN	UNFELT	UNCONFESSED	WHOLE TRUTH
ACKNOWLEDGEMENT	COMFORT	CLOTHING	FOUNDATION

My expectation is from him.
—Psalm 62:5

It is the believer's privilege to use this language. If he is looking for anything from the world, it is a poor *"expectation"* indeed. But if he looks to God for the supply of his needs, whether in temporal or spiritual blessings, his expectation will not be a vain one. Constantly, he may draw from the bank of faith and have his needs supplied out of the riches of God's lovingkindness. I know this: I would rather have God for my banker than all the Rothschilds. My Lord never fails to honor His promises. When we bring them to His throne, He never sends them back unanswered. Therefore, I will wait only at His door, for He always opens it with the hand of lavish grace. At this hour I will try Him anew. But we have expectations beyond this life. We will die soon, and then, our *"expectation is from him."* Do we not expect that when we lie on the bed of sickness He will send angels to carry us to His bosom? We believe that when the pulse is faint and the heart beats heavily, some angelic messenger will stand and look with loving eyes on us and whisper, "Sister spirit, come away!" As we approach the heavenly gate, we expect to hear the welcome invitation, *"Come, ye blessed of my Father, inherit the kingdom prepared for you from the foundation of the world"* (Matt. 25:34). We are expecting harps of gold and crowns of glory; we are hoping soon to be among the multitude of shining ones before the throne. We are looking forward and longing for the time when we will be like our glorious Lord, for *"we shall see him as he is"* (1 John 3:2). Then, if these are your expectations, O my soul, live for God. Live with the desire and resolve to glorify Him from whom come all your supplies, and of whose grace in your election, redemption, and calling, it is that you have any *"expectation"* of coming glory.

```
V F S S D A B F B Z B A N K E R A R A B
L A V I S H G R A C E U U H V H I S J S
K E B R W M Y S V V D U W U H O Y U Y P
U Q K A B L X P R O M I S E S N E P S I
E N P I N Q R T P Y U M O Q P O X P U R
G L O R N K D V E H V Q S L Q R P L P I
L J O T I H O K T M O R C J I W E Y P T
I W Q V I V E F O T P K W G Z F C O L U
S S I G I N I R F T A O M F U O T F I A
U A L Q H N V L I A H U R X W U A N E L
F N A N U U G A E T I E Y A L N T E D B
X G C S M N L K I G P T N O L D I E O L
L E E J F L G M I N E N H L O A O D F E
X L E L E C T I O N T B I J Z T N S I S
B I Q K Z R F D E P D M H N W I C O C S
Q C G Z S V Z O I W K N M J K O E I X I
R Z H O C K K Q U M N O E Q Q N T E O N
E R I C H E S F H Z A V E S A G U D V G
B E U L A N G U A G E T U D S S T U D S
B E L I E V E R F K I V T P J M R V K B
```

EXPECTATION	BELIEVER	PRIVILEGE	LANGUAGE
SUPPLY OF NEEDS	TEMPORAL	SPIRITUAL BLESSINGS	NOT IN VAIN
BANK OF FAITH	SUPPLIED	RICHES	LOVINGKINDNESS
BANKER	HONOR	PROMISES	LAVISH GRACE
ANGELIC	INHERIT	FOUNDATION	ELECTION

Morning

The barrel of meal wasted not, neither did the cruse of oil fail,
according to the word of the LORD, which he spake by Elijah.
—1 Kings 17:16

See the faithfulness of divine love. Observe that this woman had daily needs. She had to feed herself and her son during a time of famine; now, in addition, the prophet Elijah needed to be fed. But though the need was three times as great, the meal did not run out, for she had a constant supply. Each day she went to the barrel, but each day the amount in it remained the same. You, dear reader, also have daily needs. Because they come so frequently, you are inclined to fear that the barrel of meal will one day be empty, and the jar of oil will fail you. Rest assured that, according to the Word of God, this will not be the case. Each day, though it brings its troubles, will also bring its help. Though you would live to outnumber the years of Methuselah, and your needs would be as numerous as the sands of the seashore, God's grace and mercy will last through all your necessities, and you will never know a real lack. For three long years during this widow's lifetime, the heavens never saw a cloud, and the stars never wept a holy tear of dew upon the wicked earth. Famine, desolation, and death made the land a howling wilderness, but this woman was never hungry; she was always joyful in abundance. So will it be for you. You will see the sinner's hope perish, for he trusts in his own strength. You will see the proud Pharisee's confidence waver, for he builds his hope on the sand. You will even see your own schemes blasted and withered, but you will find that your place of defense will be in the Rock of your salvation. Your bread will be given to you, and your water supply will be secure. It is better to have God for your guardian than to own the Bank of England. You might spend the wealth of the Indies, but you can never exhaust the infinite riches of God.

```
P L W B N S B U I K G L V N W P W T C Q
Q I I N E C E S S I T I E S O M H F H B
S F J W V T R I B J J G D J R E M A T A
L E Q A W V E E H O S S S C D T D I S R
O T P S Q O X W M E B F H T O H I T A R
U I F T B U B R J A L J C O F U V H N E
S M F E I V L S S K I P A R T S I F D L
U E C D J C P A E S J N T B H E N U S O
X C K N I M J R F R L J E N E L E L O F
D R B O F L N G O A V V I D L A L N F M
T U S T F Q E B G P A E R Y O H O E T E
E S E V T Q Y M M P H E L P R G V S H A
A E G Z H P Y N C O P E L B D A E S E L
Y O C B G V U N Z K Y Z T I S O J T S G
T F F V E J N O U M V Y I V J B K A H D
K O K I R E S T A S S U R E D A M N O A
P I C O N S T A N T S U P P L Y H H R J
V L Q N Y U G X U N U M E R O U S J E L
X G X L X D A I L Y N E E D S E U B P J
Q T I M E O F F A M I N E A I T D V Y I
```

BARREL OF MEAL	WASTED NOT	CRUSE OF OIL	WORD OF THE LORD
ELIJAH	FAITHFULNESS	DIVINE LOVE	OBSERVE
DAILY NEEDS	TIME OF FAMINE	PROPHET	CONSTANT SUPPLY
REMAINED	REST ASSURED	HELP	METHUSELAH
NUMEROUS	SANDS OF THE SHORE	NECESSITIES	LIFETIME

 Evening

Awake, O north wind; and come, thou south; blow upon my garden,
that the spices thereof may flow out.
—Song of Solomon 4:16

Anything is better than the dead calm of indifference. Our souls may wisely desire the north wind of trouble if that alone can be sanctified to the drawing forth of the perfume of our graces. As long as it cannot be said, "*The LORD was not in the wind*" (1 Kings 19:11), we will not shrink from the wintriest blast that ever blew on plants of grace. Did not the spouse in this verse humbly submit herself to the reproofs of her Beloved? Did she not entreat Him to send forth His grace in some form and make no stipulation as to the particular manner in which it should come? Did she not, like ourselves, become so utterly weary of deadness and unholy calm that she sighed for any visitation that would brace her to action? Yet she desired the warm south wind of comfort, too, the smiles of divine love, the joy of the Redeemer's presence. These are often mightily effective in arousing our sluggish life. She desired either one or the other, or both, so that she might be able to delight her Beloved with the spices of her garden. She could not endure to be unprofitable, nor can we. How cheering a thought that Jesus can find comfort in our poor feeble graces. Can it be? It seems far too good to be true. Well may we court trial or even death itself if we will thereby be aided to make Immanuel's heart glad. Oh, that our hearts were crushed to atoms if only by such bruising our sweet Lord Jesus could be glorified. Graces unexercised are as sweet perfumes slumbering in the cups of flowers. The wisdom of the great Husbandman overrules diverse and opposite causes to produce the one desired result. He makes both affliction and consolation draw forth the grateful fragrances of faith, love, patience, hope, resignation, joy, and the other fair flowers of the garden. May we know, by sweet experience, what this means.

```
S  I  C  L  R  E  D  E  E  M  E  R  N  A  N  D  S  O  F  D
L  U  E  H  Q  X  M  B  O  X  Y  I  T  J  D  C  Z  T  W  N
H  U  B  C  E  M  Z  D  T  Z  A  M  D  F  V  V  D  T  L  E
J  D  X  M  V  E  I  Z  X  B  I  M  F  H  I  S  I  G  L  X
S  S  X  I  I  Q  R  E  A  M  C  A  D  B  S  Q  C  A  G  P
L  P  F  N  A  T  G  I  D  G  I  N  U  S  S  S  C  C  V  E
A  I  B  O  W  P  U  M  N  V  O  U  B  Z  N  J  T  T  S  R
I  H  N  R  I  E  Y  I  S  G  X  E  W  P  W  Q  G  I  J  I
W  I  N  T  R  Y  B  L  A  S  T  L  M  V  S  J  Z  O  O  E
R  K  O  H  E  W  V  V  I  S  I  T  A  T  I  O  N  N  U  N
L  Q  Z  W  T  Z  E  F  F  E  C  T  I  V  E  R  B  B  T  C
P  M  B  I  R  I  N  D  I  F  F  E  R  E  N  C  E  S  F  E
G  J  G  N  R  P  P  E  R  F  U  M  E  W  O  E  S  L  L  R
O  W  Z  D  H  F  A  I  R  F  L  O  W  E  R  S  P  U  O  G
H  L  D  R  C  A  O  J  T  X  J  B  Z  J  T  Z  I  T  W  A
D  N  U  J  Z  W  I  C  N  P  T  T  D  B  S  K  C  L  W  R
B  Y  D  E  A  D  C  A  L  M  G  W  N  I  Q  S  E  K  M  D
X  Y  G  J  B  A  Q  P  B  E  L  O  V  E  D  I  S  D  F  E
O  H  C  A  A  M  F  W  O  M  P  R  E  S  E  N  C  E  P  N
V  R  K  H  U  S  B  A  N  D  M  A  N  I  Z  M  S  A  A  D
```

NORTH WIND	GARDEN	SPICES	OUTFLOW
DEAD CALM	INDIFFERENCE	PERFUME	WINTRY BLAST
SUBMIT	BELOVED	VISITATION	ACTION
REDEEMER	PRESENCE	EFFECTIVE	CHEERING
IMMANUEL	HUSBANDMAN	FAIR FLOWERS	EXPERIENCE

71

Morning

He is precious.
—1 Peter 2:7

As all the rivers run into the sea, so all delights center on our Beloved. The glance of His eyes outshines the sun. The beauty of His face is fairer than the choicest flowers. No fragrance is like the breath of His mouth. Gems of the earth and pearls from the sea are worthless things when compared to His preciousness. Peter told us that Jesus is precious, but he did not and could not tell us how precious, nor could any of us compute the value of God's unspeakable gift. Words cannot express the preciousness of the Lord Jesus to His people or fully tell how essential He is to their satisfaction and happiness. Believer, have you not found in the midst of plenty a sore famine if your Lord has been absent? The sun was shining, but Christ had hidden Himself, and all the world was black to you; or it was night, and since the *"bright and morning star"* (Rev. 22:16) was gone, no other star could yield so much as a ray of light to you. What a howling wilderness this world is without our Lord! If He hides Himself from us, the flowers of our garden wither. Our pleasant fruits decay, the birds suspend their songs, and a tempest overturns our hopes. All earth's candles cannot make daylight if the Sun of Righteousness is eclipsed. He is the Soul of our souls, the Light of our light, the Life of our lives. Dear reader, what would you do in the world without Him, when you wake up and look ahead to the day's battle? What would you do at night, when you come home jaded and weary, if there were no door of fellowship between you and Christ? Blessed is His name! He will not allow us to try our lot without Him, for Jesus never forsakes His own. Yet let the thought of what life would be without Him enhance His preciousness.

```
O F B R D H Q S Q B P W P L E N T Y R J
S V G K H E N D A Y R M D K R C Q U A H
L G E G L A N C E T T I H Z O M R N J T
O N I P Y O A W X U I F G X P M I D G F
K Y O D E L I G H T S S T H W O V T A R
W E B Z D T P X J D H V F G T J E I V A
G H W I J V C V O Z J R J A P W R U P G
X N H P S C Z N A K P L E M C Y S I T R
C F B E A U T Y R L G Y N V F T N Y Z A
O G L P B J T L I Q U S I W Z P I H R N
M C B C Y J N S E W H E Y T N W M O P C
P W S I W A M O R N I N G S T A R P N E
U O U T S H I N E S A Y P B G F N E C A
T R G V S H J C I Z E X G N V U F A L B
E U H A P P I N E S S X B V Y B A R M C
R J E S S E N T I A L C F F D Q I L A G
R U N S P E A K A B L E G I F T R S F J
G P W L M S L K T O T H E S E A E T M V
C H R N R Y P R E C I O U S Y J R F S R
E C L U L G E M S O F T H E E A R T H V
```

PRECIOUS	RIVERS	TO THE SEA	DELIGHTS
GLANCE	OUTSHINES	BEAUTY	FAIRER
FRAGRANCE	GEMS OF THE EARTH	PEARLS	COMPUTE
VALUE	UNSPEAKABLE GIFT	ESSENTIAL	SATISFACTION
HAPPINESS	PLENTY	BRIGHT	MORNING STAR

Evening

Unto me, who am less than the least of all saints, is this grace given, that I should preach among the Gentiles the unsearchable riches of Christ.
—Ephesians 3:8

The apostle Paul felt it was a great privilege to be allowed to preach the Gospel. He did not look on his calling as a drudgery, but he fulfilled it with intense delight. Yet while Paul was thankful for his calling, his success in it greatly humbled him. The fuller a vessel becomes, the deeper it sinks in the water. Idlers may indulge a fond conceit of their abilities, because they are untried; but the earnest worker soon learns his own weakness. If you seek humility, try hard work. If you would know your nothingness, attempt some great thing for Jesus. If you would feel how utterly powerless you are apart from the living God, attempt the great work of proclaiming *the unsearchable riches of Christ,* and you will know, as you never knew before, what a weak, unworthy thing you are. Although the apostle thus knew and confessed his weakness, he was never perplexed as to the subject of his ministry. From his first sermon to his last, Paul preached Christ, and nothing but Christ. He lifted up the cross and extolled the Son of God who bled thereon. Follow his example in all your personal efforts to spread the glad tidings of salvation, and let "Christ and Him crucified" (see 1 Corinthians 2:2) be your ever-recurring theme. The Christian should be like those lovely spring flowers that, when the sun is shining, open their golden cups, as if to say, "Fill us with your beams!" but when the sun is hidden behind a cloud, they close their cups and droop their heads. Likewise, the Christian should feel the sweet influence of Jesus. Jesus must be his sun, and he must be the flower that yields itself to the Sun of Righteousness. Oh, to speak of Christ alone is the subject that is both *seed to the sower, and bread to the eater*" (Isa. 55:10). This is the live coal for the lips of the speaker and the master key to the heart of the hearer.

```
U N T I R E D O V U P P N M U E H U E E
O L G U X R K B S N V Q V A N S L S A C
B E B X G O N W U S N R D P Q N W X R H
I A Q F R W Q J C E K G W O D Y K C N R
M S M Q E Z Q X C A Z P L S U X C A E I
N T Y Y A E R D E R Q E T T C V A U S S
F O Q I T G V H S C Q R I L W O J U T T
J F K E T G Q L S H F P M E T V U D S C
D A U L H Q D W H A M L A P M G I Y T R
C L X D I D H A H B D E S A Q W M Q Y U
P L D P N L A V A L B X T U G O R W D C
R S I R G L I U Y E J E E L X D C U R I
O D H E N B R V W R Q D R V H V M V U F
C E R A E R R E E I J X K D U S B O D I
L L J C H M V S M C F M E W M A B G G E
A I C H L O K S W H O A Y C B W U V E D
I G V L K E K E F E Z A K Z L J A H R O
M H Q E R X Y L Y S Y E L T E I T C Y M
Q T T H A N K F U L B R T W D I G K E B
L I T N O T H I N G N E S S C J E H T G
```

LEAST OF ALL	UNSEARCHABLE RICHES	APOSTLE PAUL	PREACH
DRUDGERY	DELIGHT	THANKFUL	SUCCESS
HUMBLED	VESSEL	UNTIRED	EARNEST
NOTHINGNESS	GREAT THING	PROCLAIM	PERPLEXED
CHRIST CRUCIFIED	YIELD	LIVE COAL	MASTER KEY

Morning

Ye must be born again.
—John 3:7

Regeneration is a subject that lies at the very basis of salvation, and we should be very diligent to take heed that we really are *"born again,"* for there are many who imagine they are, who are not. Be assured that the name of a Christian is not the nature of a Christian; and that being born in a Christian land and being recognized as professing the Christian religion is of no avail whatever unless there is something more added to it—being born again is a matter so mysterious that human words cannot describe it. *"The wind bloweth where it listeth, and thou hearest the sound thereof, but canst not tell whence it cometh, and whither it goeth: so is every one that is born of the Spirit"* (John 3:8). Nevertheless, it is a change that is known and felt: known by works of holiness and felt by a gracious experience. This great work is supernatural. It is not an operation that a man performs for himself. A new principle is infused, which works in the heart, renews the soul, and affects the entire man. It is not a change of my name, but a renewal of my nature, so that I am not the person I used to be, but a *"new creature"* (2 Cor. 5:17) in Christ Jesus. To wash and dress a corpse is a far different thing from making it alive. Man can do the one, but God alone can do the other. If you have, then, been born again, your acknowledgment will be, "O Lord Jesus, the everlasting Father, You are my spiritual Parent. Unless Your Spirit had breathed into me the breath of a new, holy, spiritual life, I would have been to this day *'dead in trespasses and sins'* (Eph. 2:1). My heavenly life is wholly derived from You, and from You alone. My *'life is hid with Christ in God'* (Col. 3:3). It is no longer I who live, but Christ who lives in me (Gal. 2:20)." May the Lord enable us to be well assured on this vital point, for to be unregenerate is to be unsaved, unpardoned, without God, and without hope.

```
I D S E G F L K W G U L G T I Q L F B F
B C D V R J D M O U Z J Q Z K B K Q A J
S V W L R K B H R W V R M P V O B P S R
E D Z U E H F I K T V E N N U V O R I X
E C M V N M G N O L G G D I M S R O S N
A X N Q E Z T F F U M E C P I U N F O U
W E A R W G U U H S J N H R M P A E F D
E K T W S S T S O S P E R I A E G S S R
V L U Y H W J S L Y R R I N G R A S A E
E T R T D A M E I L T A S C I N I I L P
R G E E E N T D N I Z T T I N A N N V E
L Q Z M T D T Y E Y S I I P E T J G A R
A N Q I R D G B S Y U O A L R U M P T I
S N J X O D P B S S Z N N E P R U B I E
T D U N Z U Z R R C X H V Q D A W N O N
I B M Y S T E R I O U S N W K L U J N C
N A D C W A S S U R E D I L I G E N T E
G T N Z P Q F X R E L I G I O N L H K N
T G R A C I O U S R Y B B Z Q O L M D F
G S W S D E S C R I B E B Y I Z K V Y M
```

BORN AGAIN	REGENERATION	BASIS OF SALVATION	DILIGENT
IMAGINE	ASSURED	NATURE	CHRISTIAN
PROFESSING	RELIGION	MYSTERIOUS	DESCRIBE
WORK OF HOLINESS	GRACIOUS	EXPERIENCE	SUPERNATURAL
PRINCIPLE	INFUSED	RENEWS	EVERLASTING

DAY 19

Evening

Before destruction the heart of man is haughty.
—Proverbs 18:12

It is an old, familiar saying that "coming events cast their shadows before them." The writer of Proverbs teaches us that a haughty heart is the prophetic prelude to evil. Pride forecasts destruction even more reliably than a change of mercury in the barometer predicts rain. When men have ridden the high horse, destruction has always overtaken them. Let David's aching heart show that there is an eclipse of a man's glory when he focuses on his own greatness. (See 2 Samuel 24:10.) Nebuchadnezzar, the mighty builder of Babylon, was reduced to creeping on the earth, devouring grass like an ox, until his nails had grown like birds' claws and his hair like eagles' feathers. (See Daniel 4:33.) Pride turned the boaster into a beast, just as once before it had made an angel into a devil. God hates haughty looks and never fails to bring them down. All the arrows of God are aimed at proud hearts. Christian, is your heart haughty this evening? For pride can get into the Christian's heart as well as into the sinner's; it can delude him into dreaming that he is *rich, and increased with goods, and* [in] *need of nothing* (Rev. 3:17). Are you glorying in your grace or your talents? Are you proud of yourself because you have a holy expression and sweet experiences? If so, then, take note, reader: destruction is coming to you also. Your flaunting poppies of self-conceit will be pulled up by the roots, your mushroom graces will wither in the burning heat, and your self-sufficiency will become as straw for the dunghill. If we forget to live at the foot of the cross in deepest lowliness of spirit, God will not forget to make us suffer under His rod. Destruction will come to you, O self-exalted believer. The destruction of your joys and of your comforts will come, even though there can be no destruction of your soul. Therefore, *"he that glorieth, let him glory in the Lord"* (1 Cor. 1:31).

```
H B E R B U H A U G H T Y C X Y X C G M
T U L V B O L W A G X W H E Z M L H Q M
J R Y H E D A L N J L B W H U I C G N A
B N W Z A O N S J N M A J O N G C B E P
H I U C S Z I P T F H R N L S H P N B R
S N T D T X R R L E T O T Y D T X U U O
L G X O A F K E W E R M K E E Y A C C V
M H L F H E C L I P S E K X V B L X H E
N E L H O I P U F G E T H P I U H A A R
J A T T Y C D D H P Z E F R L I R N D B
I T B S O W U E L V F R Z E I L H G N S
T E X B M E R C U R Y C C S D D G E E O
O E Q C V E R A U A R B K S V E L L Z K
X E A R R O W S O F G O D I M R O T Z W
R Z T K O F Q U C O Y E K O U M R Z A H
K P A N C X P C S H K S K N E V Y N R R
V T Z Q D E S T R U C T I O N B D I J Z
V Z U W M C D E L H I G H H O R S E Q Z
J X F Y Q B E F H A S B A B Y L O N E N
F Q H C S O N H E A R T O F M A N W K S
```

HEART OF MAN	PROVERBS	HAUGHTY	PRELUDE
DESTRUCTION	MERCURY	BAROMETER	HIGH HORSE
ECLIPSE	NEBUCHADNEZZAR	MIGHTY BUILDER	BABYLON
BOASTER	BEAST	ANGEL	DEVIL
ARROWS OF GOD	HOLY EXPRESSION	BURNING HEAT	GLORY

Morning

Let him that thinketh he standeth take heed lest he fall.
—1 Corinthians 10:12

It is a curious fact that there is such a thing as being proud of grace. A man says, "I have great faith; I will not fall. Poor, Little-faith may, but I never will." "I have fervent love," says another. "I can stand; there is no danger of my going astray." He who boasts of grace has little grace of which to boast. Some who do this imagine that their graces can keep them, knowing not that the stream must flow constantly from the fountainhead, or else the brook will soon be dry. If a continuous stream of oil does not come to the lamp, though it burns brightly today, it will smoke tomorrow, and its scent will be noxious. Take heed that you do not glory in your graces, but let all your glorying and confidence be in Christ and His strength, for only then can you be kept from falling. Pray much. Spend longer times in holy adoration. Read the Scriptures more earnestly and constantly. Watch your lives more carefully. Live nearer to God. Take the best examples for your pattern. Let your conversation be holy. Let your hearts be perfumed with affection for men's souls. Live in such a way that men will know that you have been with Jesus and have learned of Him. When that happy day will come, when He whom you love will say, "Come up higher," may it be your happiness to hear Him say, "[You] *have fought a good fight, [you] have finished [your] course, [you] have kept the faith: henceforth there is laid up for [you] a crown of righteousness*" (2 Tim. 4:7–8). On, Christian, with care and caution! On, with holy fear and trembling! On, with faith and confidence in Jesus alone, and let your constant petition be, "*Uphold me according unto thy word*" (Ps. 119:116). He is able, and He alone, "*to keep you from falling, and to present you faultless before the presence of his glory with exceeding joy*" (Jude 24).

```
Y C S C R I P T U R E S S E O I X L N P
A I Q Q X B R T G L O R Y C N K B Q M V
P D P K R W P E P J I H M D E I H J C Z
A J X O G J R M T Q D K F Q L P O X H P
K W N X S U A S U A H B G G Z T L V R Z
B Z J A W R Y L A R K Z I L H E Y R I P
R R U Y M U M F W V T E B Z E T A G S C
L Z O T F O U N T A I N H E A D D E T I
I D L O Q W C X X H V T H E K P O G S A
V Q O B K Q H L T X O K Y O E C R O S C
E Z B O A S T O F G R A C E L D A W T O
N G J B U R N B R I G H T L Y C T L R N
E P F L O W C O N S T A N T L Y I A E F
A T Y L P P L J L X F O T Q Z R O M N I
R D Q S T R E A M O F O I L S T N P G D
V I Y N Y Y L E S T H E F A L L F D T E
M I H O L Y C O N V E R S A T I O N H N
T H I N K S H E S T A N D S B Y W T F C
T R Y C O X R M L U X H K O K H U T I E
C U R I O U S F E R V E N T L O V E R D
```

THINKS HE STANDS	TAKE HEED	LEST HE FALL	CURIOUS
FERVENT LOVE	BOAST OF GRACE	FLOW CONSTANTLY	FOUNTAINHEAD
BROOK	STREAM OF OIL	LAMP	BURN BRIGHTLY
GLORY	CONFIDENCE	CHRIST'S STRENGTH	PRAY MUCH
HOLY ADORATION	SCRIPTURES	LIVE NEAR	HOLY CONVERSATION

Evening

I will take heed to my ways.
—Psalm 39:1

Fellow pilgrim, do not say in your heart, "I will go here and there, and I will not sin," for you are never so far from the danger of sinning as to boast of security. The road is very muddy; it will be hard to pick your path so as not to soil your garments. This world is full of corruption; you will need to watch often if, in handling it, you are to keep yourself clean. At every turn in the road, there is a thief ready to rob you of your jewels. There is a temptation in every blessing and a snare in every joy. If you ever reach heaven, it will be a miracle of divine grace to be ascribed entirely to your Father's power. Be on your guard. When a man carries an explosive in his hands, he should be careful not to go near an open flame. You, too, must take care that you do not enter into temptation. Even your daily activities are sharp tools; you must watch how you handle them. There is nothing in this world to foster a Christian's faith, but everything tries to destroy it. How quick you should be to look to God so that He may keep you! Your prayer should be, "Hold me up, and I will be safe." Having prayed, you must also watch; guard every thought, word, and action with holy jealousy. Do not expose yourselves unnecessarily to danger, but if you are called to go where the darts are flying, never venture forth without your shield. If even once the devil finds you without protection, he will rejoice that his hour of triumph has come, and he will soon make you fall down wounded by his arrows. Though you cannot be slain, you can be wounded. Be sober; be vigilant. Danger may come in the hour when everything seems to be the most secure. Therefore, take heed to your ways, and pray diligently. No one ever fell into error through being too watchful. May the Holy Spirit guide us in all our ways so that we may always please the Lord.

```
D L M C D B A W Z L L U Y Q Q B G K H D
W I W D O U S A M J Y L V B Q L F E Y A
G H V A L R Y V A S O J M O E E R P S N
Q A G I T F R P I L G R I M U S P T F G
O R R K N C O U B S J L A E E S J C J E
R B J M B E H A P E S J R Y V I T L E R
R V T O E O G F L T B Y Q A E N P E W O
S O H E Y N A R U P I I G L R G T A E F
T E X B M N T S A L G O D Z Y M A N L S
X L C R Y P S S T C U P N F T N T C S I
O T Y U S B T T V P E B X W H C Z B V N
N C A M R R F A T H E R S P O W E R O N
M T C Y U I N V T S S G O X U R T P E I
E U N I D W T H L I Q H N O G Q W R Q N
H G Q Z G A R Y V G O E G T H C E R W G
D I L I G E N T L Y U N U F T B U W G N
H U Q R J N R V A M B A A I S N A R E P
U W D I O B A L I B Y A R E V G K E H R
N V Q P L Q U T A A E L D D E Z J G Y T
K V F L J V C T A K E C A R E T E A J R
```

PILGRIM	DANGER OF SINNING	BOAST	SECURITY
GARMENTS	CORRUPTION	KEPT CLEAN	JEWELS
TEMPTATION	BLESSING	SNARE	JOY
DIVINE GRACE	FATHER'S POWER	ON GUARD	TAKE CARE
GUARD	EVERY THOUGHT	DILIGENTLY	WATCHFUL

Morning

Be strong in the grace that is in Christ Jesus.
—2 Timothy 2:1

Christ has grace without measure in Himself, but He has not retained it for Himself. As the reservoir empties itself into the pipes, so has Christ emptied out His grace for His people. *"Of his fulness have all we received, and grace for grace"* (John 1:16). He seems only to have in order to dispense to us. He stands like the fountain, always flowing, but only running in order to supply the empty pitchers and the thirsty lips that draw near to it. Like a tree, He bears sweet fruit, not to hang on boughs, but to be gathered by those who have need. Grace, whether its work is to pardon, to cleanse, to preserve, to strengthen, to enlighten, to quicken, or to restore, is ever to be had from Him freely and without price. Nor is there one form of the work of grace that He has not bestowed on His people. As the blood of the body, though flowing from the heart, belongs equally to every member, so the influences of grace are the inheritance of every saint united to the Lamb. Herein there is a sweet communion between Christ and His church, inasmuch as they both receive the same grace. Christ is the Head on which the oil is first poured, but the same oil runs to the very skirts of the garments, so that the humblest saint has an unction of the same costly moisture as that which fell on the Head. This is true communion when the sap of grace flows from the stem to the branch, and when it is perceived that the stem itself is sustained by the very nourishment that feeds the branch. As we day by day receive grace from Jesus, and more constantly recognize it as coming from Him, we will behold Him in communion with us, and enjoy communion with Him. Let us make daily use of our riches and ever go to Him as to our own Lord in covenant, taking from Him the supply of all we need with as much boldness as men take money from their own pockets.

```
S V E O W O R P S R G M R P Y P D N S B
D T Q G C I O E T D T S V T C H C O V E
V U R N J I T R S Y A C H W J P H A H S
C T Q E A N E H H E L C M S A F R C C T
E U R L N V Z Q O P R Q W A S U I L P O
X N O E G G Z R U U Y V T F X L S E I W
D A L Q T S T K E A T C O E R L T A P E
H Q Z I X A T H B C L M I I G N J N E D
O C I C G Y I D E F I L E T R E E S S U
X O R L T H L N E N P E Y A W S S E U I
M W I Q J I T X E G A R V B S S U Z F K
V U A H Q Z V E O D Y W E E I U S B J V
T E V K T X D E N C V R Y S D G R D N T
L Q M F B N S P A R D O N F E C L E Q L
V W H R J J N Q U I C K E N E R K Q C L
P S T V C F R E S T O R E F C B V N B D
N J J M S T R O N G I N G R A C E E Q H
U P I N H I M S E L F Q E C P A B M W T
E E I Q L U L Y I V E M P T I E D R T H
Q W I T H O U T P R I C E F K A P K C L
```

STRONG IN GRACE	CHRIST JESUS	WITHOUT MEASURE	IN HIMSELF
RETAINED	RESERVOIR	EMPTIED	PIPES
FULLNESS	RECEIVED	PARDON	CLEANSE
PRESERVE	STRENGTHEN	ENLIGHTEN	QUICKEN
RESTORE	WITHOUT PRICE	BESTOWED	EQUALLY

Evening

I am a stranger with thee.
—Psalm 39:12

O Lord, I am a stranger *with* You, but not *to* You. All my natural alienation from You, Your grace has effectively removed. Now, in fellowship with You, I walk through this sinful world as a pilgrim in a foreign country. Lord, You are a stranger in Your own world. Man forgets You, dishonors You, sets up new laws and alien customs, and does not know You. When Your dear Son came to His own, His own did not receive Him (John 1:11). *"He was in the world, and the world was made by him, and the world knew him not"* (v. 10). Never was a foreigner considered as questionable a character as much as Your beloved Son was among His own people. It is no surprise, then, if I who live the life of Jesus am a stranger here below. Lord, I would not be a citizen where Jesus was an alien. His pierced hand has loosened the cords that once bound my soul to earth, and now I find myself a stranger in the land. Among those with whom I dwell, my speech seems to these an outlandish tongue, my manners unusual, and my actions strange. A barbarian would be more at home among genteel society than I could ever be among the company of sinners. But here is the sweetness of my lot: I am a stranger along with You. You are my fellow sufferer, my fellow pilgrim. Oh, what joy to be in such blessed society! My heart burns within me by the way when You speak to me, and though I am a sojourner, I am far more blessed than those who sit on thrones or dwell in their comfortable houses.

> To me remains nor place, nor time:
> My country is in every clime;
> I can be calm and free from care
> On any shore, since God is there.
> While place we seek, or place we shun,
> The soul finds happiness in none:
> But with a God to guide our way,
> 'Tis equal joy to go or stay.

```
W W S R H K R S O B L O O S E N E D I T
H A P P I N E S S W D Z X S X M Y A Q E
C J L X G E C I T I Z E N P S F E L M J
S J I Y F G E U C I G W F H Z V L I S C
Y I X R W P L Z B P Q J D M A C T E K A
L D X H G H I S O W N E X A Z K H N S F
H L E A J B E E L W Q R F N V M I A K O
X O M K B W E P R O K A S N U C S T S R
B C P X Q R H T K C V V M E C O P I O G
S T R A N G E R C A E N T R A R I O J O
E L H O R L U A K I M D N S R D L N O T
G Q K H U Z H W L J H O H H K S G X U T
B O U N D E L S I J K N S A U U R T R E
Q Y Q U E S T I O N A B L E N R I A N N
D F F H U E A H H O K J Q G A D M J E N
S K L N J C H E R E B E L O W Q C F R T
W F O R E I G N C O U N T R Y Y E U U N
B J P I R Z Q L F E L L O W S H I P I V
N C H A R A C T E R R E M O V E D R I N
S K X M C Q I D U D I S H O N O R E D Q
```

STRANGER	ALIENATION	REMOVED	FELLOWSHIP
PILGRIM	FOREIGN COUNTRY	FORGOTTEN	DISHONORED
HIS OWN	QUESTIONABLE	CHARACTER	HERE BELOW
CITIZEN	PIERCED HAND	LOOSENED	CORDS
BOUND	MANNERS	SOJOURNER	HAPPINESS

Morning

Keep back thy servant also from presumptuous sins.
—Psalm 19:13

Such was the prayer of David, the *"man after [God's] own heart"* (Acts 13:22). If holy David needed to pray this way, how much more do we, babes in grace, need to do so! It is as if he said, "Keep me back, or I will rush headlong over the precipice of sin." Our evil natures, like an ill-tempered horse, are prone to run away. May the grace of God put the bridle on them and hold them in, so that we do not rush into mischief. What might the best of us not do if it were not for the boundaries that the Lord sets upon us both in providence and in grace? The psalmist's prayer is directed against the worst form of sin—that which is done with deliberation and willfulness. Even the holiest need to be "kept back" from the vilest transgressions. It is a solemn thing to find the apostle Paul warning saints against the most loathsome sins. *"Mortify therefore your members which are upon the earth; fornication, uncleanness, inordinate affection, evil concupiscence, and covetousness, which is idolatry"* (Col. 3:5). What! Do saints need to be warned against such sins as these? Yes, they do. The whitest robes, unless their purity is preserved by divine grace, will be defiled by the blackest spots. Experienced Christian, do not boast in your experience; you will trip if you look away from Him who *"is able to keep you from falling"* (Jude 24). You whose love is fervent, whose faith is constant, whose hopes are bright, do not say, "We will never sin." Instead, cry, *"Lead us not into temptation"* (Matt. 6:13). There is enough kindling in the heart of the best of men to light a fire that will burn to the lowest hell, unless God quenches the sparks as they fall. Who would have dreamed that righteous Lot could have been found drunken and committing uncleanness? Hazael said, *"Is thy servant a dog, that he should do this great thing?"* (2 Kings 8:13). We are very likely to ask the same self-righteous question. May infinite wisdom cure us of the foolishness of self-confidence.

```
K D A D L N N R N S J B D M C I B J J Q
D T F L E F S W U P V U W J P A R H O P
I C Z B L L F E I S A D J C U C I O J Q
B A J D P K I R T L H U U L V V D L B P
A B C L R W P B C C L H Q W N P L Y A R
B F K C C G G F E O Y F E Y S T E D G E
E F E R V E N T U R N F U A N L C A U S
S P R E C I P I C E A S W L D E W V M U
I P E R S E V E R E D T T F N L V I S M
N K A B W W K I C E W D I A W E O D Z P
G N K Z H D W P M V A R G O N W S N M T
R X E A G M M D F T K W D A N T W S G U
A F E W D F M Z T L S O L E M N A Y M O
C L P Y T U N I G O K I U Q Z P R S G U
E J B W P T H Y S E R V A N T U N K C S
Q Z A A J X L U L B R I G H T R I K U A
E D C P P B W K Y Q C W V O X I N F D C
F W K X B O U N D A R I E S N T G G Q X
W N Y Z M I S C H I E F X P Q Y G I W R
W H I T E S T R O B E S E K H M E P Z M
```

KEEP BACK	THY SERVANT	PRESUMPTUOUS	HOLY DAVID
BABES IN GRACE	RUSH HEADLONG	PRECIPICE	BRIDLE
MISCHIEF	BOUNDARIES	DELIBERATION	WILLFULNESS
SOLEMN	WARNING	WHITEST ROBES	PURITY
PERSEVERED	FERVENT	CONSTANT	BRIGHT

DAY 22

Evening

And she said, Truth, Lord: yet the dogs eat of the crumbs
which fall from their masters' table.
—Matthew 15:27

This woman gained comfort in her misery by thinking great thoughts of Christ. The Master had talked about the children's bread. "Now," she reasoned, "since You are the Master of the table of grace, I know that You are a generous Host. There is sure to be abundance of bread on Your table. There will be more than enough food for the children—enough that there will be crumbs to throw on the floor for the dogs. The children will still have plenty even though the dogs are fed." She thought of Jesus as One who had such an abundance to give that all she needed would be just a crumb in comparison. Remember that what she really wanted was to have the devil cast out of her daughter. It was a very great thing to her, but she had such high esteem of Christ that she said, "It is nothing to Him; it is but a crumb for Christ to give. My sins are many, but it is nothing for Jesus to take them all away. The weight of my guilt presses me down as a giant's foot crushes a worm, but it is no more than a grain of dust to Him. He has already borne its curse *'in his own body on the tree'* (1 Pet. 2:24). It will be a small thing for Him to give me full remission, although it will be an infinite blessing for me to receive it." The woman opened her soul's mouth very wide, expecting great things of Jesus, and He filled it with His love. Dear reader, do the same. She confessed what Christ laid at her door, but she laid hold of Him and drew arguments even out of His hard words. She believed great things of Him, and thus she persuaded Him. She won the victory by believing in Him. Her case is an example of prevailing faith. If we would conquer like her, we must imitate her tactics. This is the royal road to comfort. Great thoughts of your sin alone will drive you to despair, but great thoughts of Christ will pilot you into the haven of peace.

```
Q W U O S L F U L L R E M I S S I O N F
U R H I G H E S T E E M F Y G E L D B T
E A B U N D A N C E E N O U G H P Z J X
D N L D W R C K K K M Z S J M A R T B I
U T X K D A P W C R U M B S I I C I O F
J W F R X D T Y N U E O E A N S H A R P
G G P Y V I B D M V T E B S F L I M N A
R S E L L A I D H O L D P A I C L A E L
V S L N E Z S Q Z D N J K W N O D S T L
R V X L E N J N L S O C H H I M R T H S
S B J X A R T M F K T T P C T F E E E H
Z D L Q D U O Y E U H B Q R E O N R C E
D U W I D Q J U H N I O U A C R S S U N
A O K Y D H M S S X N J I G V T B T R E
D O G G V F S U R A G Q X V N I R A S E
W T T S V B L E S S I N G T V N E B E D
P W Y K E J T N B Q K T Z M J V A L G E
V M F V T A B L E O F G R A C E D E M D
R L I Z T B T D F Y J H S K T F X R S O
H O S T W G R A I N O F D U S T X P V O
```

DOGS EAT	CRUMBS	MASTER'S TABLE	COMFORT
CHILDREN'S BREAD	TABLE OF GRACE	GENEROUS	HOST
ABUNDANCE	ENOUGH	PLENTY	ALL SHE NEEDED
HIGH ESTEEM	NOTHING	GRAIN OF DUST	BORNE THE CURSE
FULL REMISSION	INFINITE	BLESSING	LAID HOLD

Morning

Let him kiss me with the kisses of his mouth.
—Song of Solomon 1:2

For several days we have been dwelling on the Savior's passion, and for some little time to come we will linger there. In beginning a new month, let us seek the same desires after our Lord as those that glowed in the heart of the elect spouse. See how she leaps at once to Him; there are no prefatory words; she does not even mention His name; she is in the heart of her theme at once, for she speaks of Him who was the only *"him"* in the world to her. How bold is her love! It was great condescension that permitted the weeping penitent to anoint His feet with spikenard. It was rich love that allowed the gentle Mary to sit at His feet and learn of Him. But here, love, strong, fervent love, aspires to higher tokens of regard and closer signs of fellowship. Esther trembled in the presence of Ahasuerus, but the spouse in joyful liberty of perfect love knows no fear. If we have received the same free spirit, we also may ask the same. By *"kisses"* we suppose to be intended those varied manifestations of affection by which the believer is made to enjoy the love of Jesus. The kiss of reconciliation we enjoyed at our conversion, and it was sweet as honey dripping from the comb. The kiss of acceptance is still warm on our brow, as we know that He has accepted our persons and our works through rich grace. The kiss of daily, present communion is what we pant after to be repeated day after day, until it is changed into the kiss of reception, which removes the soul from earth, and the kiss of consummation, which fills it with the joy of heaven. Faith is our walk, but fellowship intensely felt is our rest. Faith is the road, but communion with Jesus is the well from which the pilgrim drinks. O Lover of our souls, do not be a stranger to us; let the lips of Your blessing meet the lips of our asking. Let the lips of Your fullness touch the lips of our need, and immediately, we will feel the healing effect of Your kiss.

```
Y F J A L R N Q D S D G X M H Z F B N P
B L L H W D F C A M A F F E C T I O N N
O F R A W F E R Y E F H F S C I F H E N
L L I S Z X L A A N L Q J A R F L Z O U
D I V U B Z L W F V I V U M N R F S U C
N N D E N U O Y T T R L P E P E M J G O
E G Q R J C W H E J F C Z D S E P N C N
S E H U V H S N R P T S G E P S C E H V
S R B S D E H P D A S N T S I P F S G E
O Q E A H A I R A S L X I I K I A T M R
Z A A O P R P F Y S J T C R E R K H Y S
E O H K V T O N W I T Q O E N I V E F I
S I W Z T G K Z P O C J M S A T T R Y O
H O N E Y C O M B N K O M R R F M K V N
Y H S E L Z Z S U J I T U M D Y K I R B
Y R A I S D P Z R P E V N L C R T S E W
S I T A T H I S F E E T I U B X X S W J
V R Z V N E L E C T S P O U S E A M S P
L E A P S Q W T Q O R P N U H Q W E Y U
W R E C O N C I L I A T I O N X J M D S
```

KISS ME	PASSION	LINGER	SAME DESIRES
ELECT SPOUSE	LEAPS	HEART	BOLDNESS
SPIKENARD	SIT AT HIS FEET	ESTHER	AHASUERUS
FREE SPIRIT	AFFECTION	RECONCILIATION	CONVERSION
HONEYCOMB	COMMUNION	DAY AFTER DAY	FELLOWSHIP

93

Evening

It is time to seek the Lord.
—Hosea 10:12

This month of April is said to derive its name from the Latin verb *aperio*, which means to we have arrived at the gates of the flowery season. Reader, if you are yet unsaved, may your heart, in accord with the universal awakening of nature, be opened to receive the Lord. Every blossoming flower warns you that *"it is time to seek the Lord."* Do not be out of tune with nature, but let your heart bud and bloom with holy desires. Do you tell me that the warm blood of youth leaps in your veins? Then I entreat you, give your vigor to the Lord. It was my unspeakable happiness to be called in early youth, and I could gladly praise the Lord for it every day. Salvation is priceless; let it come when it may, but oh, an early salvation has a double value in it. Young men and women, since you may perish before you reach your prime, now is the time to seek the Lord. You who are experiencing the first signs of aging, quicken your pace. That hollow cough and hectic flush are warnings that you must not take lightly. It is indeed *"time to seek the Lord."* Did I observe a little gray mingled with your once luxurious, dark tresses? Years are swiftly passing, and death is drawing nearer with its hasty march. Let each return of spring inspire you to set your house in order. Dear reader, if you are now advanced in age, let me entreat and implore you to delay no longer. There is a day of grace for you now—be thankful for that, but it is a limited season and grows shorter every time the clock ticks. Here in your silent room, on this first night of another month, I speak to you as best I can by paper and ink. From my inmost soul, as God's servant, I lay before you this warning, *"It is time to seek the Lord."* Do not neglect that work. It may be your last call from destruction, the final syllable from the lips of grace.

```
H N G X M Q F U S Y L L A B L E X S A G
S O H M I V O L F Q D T K W E J I B R X
F Y P X Y O K Y A U C W C K I W Z L R W
X E O B P S E A S O N A J K L U I O I L
W D T U S T P Q M T L I M I T E D S V C
A Z D Y T O N F A W E F M K Z U E S E C
O D C X W H T W P H J F P K H Y L O D E
U U V L F N G D D X W T V E V S A M W W
H J T A U I H A S T Y M A R C H Y I W T
O D E O N X C M R H F V I G O R N N W W
L I S W F C U I I U D Q Q Q G S O G C H
Y G M X C T E R B I K G T L E G L T W C
D S T V C Y U D I V U L Z I Y I O Q W M
E U D N R J M N K O V Y L H U W N U U I
S U O P E N E D E O U O K M S U G I G N
I R V D Q C H W A H Q S Z V L H E C Z G
R W A R N I N G H E C T I C K K R K P L
E B Y N K X I P J G N W P C L K L E M E
S R W W A E S E E K T H E L O R D N Q D
K O I W E A R L Y E K K U T Q W B W G Z
```

SEEK THE LORD	ARRIVED	OPENED	BLOSSOMING
OUT OF TUNE	HOLY DESIRES	YOUTH	VIGOR
EARLY	QUICKEN	HECTIC	MINGLED
LUXURIOUS	HASTY MARCH	ADVANCED	DELAY NO LONGER
LIMITED	SEASON	SYLLABLE	WARNING

Morning

Come ye, and let us go up to the mountain of the LORD.
—Isaiah 2:3

It is exceedingly beneficial to our souls to rise above this present evil world to something nobler and better. The cares of this world and the deceitfulness of riches are likely to choke everything that is good within us and cause us to grow fretful, despondent, and perhaps proud and carnal. It is good for us to cut down these thorns and briers, for heavenly seed sown among them is not likely to yield a harvest. Where will we find a better sickle with which to cut them down than communion with God and the things of the kingdom? In the valleys of Switzerland, many of the inhabitants become sickly because the air is close and stagnant; but up yonder, on the mountains, you find a hardy race, who breathe the clear, fresh air as it blows from the virgin snows of the Alpine summits. It would be good if those who live in the valley could frequently leave their homes among the marshes and the fever mists and inhale the bracing mountain air. It is to such an exploit of climbing that I invite you this evening. May the Spirit of God assist us to leave the mists of fear and the fevers of anxiety and all the ills that gather in this valley of earth. Let us ascend the mountains of anticipated joy and blessedness. May God the Holy Spirit cut the cords that keep us here below and assist us to climb! Too often, we sit like chained eagles fastened to the rock. Unlike the eagle, though, we begin to love our chain and would, perhaps, if it really came to the test, loathe to have it snapped. May God grant us grace so that, if we cannot escape from the chains of our flesh, He would enable our spirits to be set free. Leaving our fleshly bodies behind, like Abraham left behind his servants when he was called to offer Isaac as a sacrifice, may our souls reach the top of the mountain. May we there enjoy communion with the Most High.

```
V E E B C O M M U N I O N O M U U S C E
O Y E M E Z V A V Z E W X R J F M A A A
T G X W H N N Q A B P Q K J X G O O R G
N U S F J O E B F I R T P N F X U E E L
V F M P R K R F J J C I S F L D N M S E
B E I D L E F E I E E I E I O J T H O T
Y V S G R Z S O C C V T U R O E A E F V
K E T I A X C H A H I U I H S C I A T T
E R S S H P W Q A A O A E W P T N V H H
I O O U D L V Q R I E K L R R O O E E O
A F F A C O O X O L R J E I E D F N W R
M A F M S D Q Z B B W G I S S F T L O N
O N E V S C O J D K F P M E E F H Y R S
S X A C S O E J N I N I H A N H E S L Q
T I R O H Z W N J S N A V B T A L E D R
H E N C B E F K D K Z V C O E R O E F I
I T J S M U T I Q M O R Q V V D R D G U
G Y P Z L E T U S G O U P E I Y D I N U
H J G G I T H A R V E S T C L B F U O M
A K W P O M V M A R S H E S U A Q O F Z
```

MOUNTAIN OF THE LORD	LET US GO UP	BENEFICIAL	RISE ABOVE
PRESENT EVIL	CARES OF THE WORLD	CHOKE	THORNS
BRIERS	HEAVENLY SEED	HARVEST	HARDY
FRESH AIR	MARSHES	MISTS OF FEAR	FEVER OF ANXIETY
ASCEND	EAGLE	COMMUNION	MOST HIGH

Evening

Let us go forth therefore unto him without the camp.
—Hebrews 13:13

Jesus, bearing His cross, went forth to suffer without the gate. The Christian's reason for leaving the camp of the world's sin and religion is not that he loves to be an individual, but because Jesus did so, and the disciple must follow his Master. Christ was *"not of the world"* (John 17:14). His life and His testimony were a constant protest against conformity with the world. Never did such overflowing affection for men exist as you find in Him, but still He was separate from sinners. Likewise, Christ's people must *"go forth…unto him."* They must take their position *"without the camp,"* as witness-bearers for the truth. They must be prepared to tread the straight and narrow path. They must have bold, unflinching, lionlike hearts, loving Christ first, and His truth next, and Christ and His truth above all the world. Jesus would have His people *"go forth…without the camp"* for their own sanctification. You cannot grow in grace to any great degree while you are conformed to the world. The life of separation may be a path of sorrow, but it is the highway of safety. And though the separated life may cost you many pangs and make every day a battle, yet it is a happy life after all. No joy can excel that of the soldier of Christ. Jesus reveals Himself so graciously and gives such sweet refreshment that the warrior feels more calm and peace in his daily strife than others feel in their hours of rest. The highway of holiness is the highway of communion. It is thus that we will hope to win the crown if we are enabled by divine grace faithfully to follow Christ *"without the camp."* The crown of glory will follow the cross of separation. A moment's shame will be well recompensed by eternal honor; a little while of witness-bearing will seem nothing when we are forever *"with the Lord"* (1 Thess. 4:17).

```
L H P M C V B U C B B S L J D T S C W F
P H A A R I E C Y A O D H S A E A I I O
L B Y S O Q A I E K U N O K M S Z T T V
K X N T W A R F Q U T T L G B T P Y N E
L P F E N S I H Z M S P I F K I G C E R
K H W R O E N K K I I T N Z F M Z O S F
A M O A F P G A I N D E E C C O G N S L
F U R F G A H J U D E W S P O N I F B O
F G L H L R I R K I T L S K O Y P O E W
E O D R O A S N F V H G I R Z X M R A I
C F S M R T C R H I E L D O V H D M R N
T O S D Y I R V Q D C P O D N D J I E G
I R I K S O O S P U A L R V I L E T R H
O T N Q Z N S V L A M W U F E O I Y B K
N H H S A I S U O L P J R V T V E K C T
P S T R A I G H T A N D N A R R O W E C
M W S F G F C O M M U N I O N O B O V P
G F J C A C D I S C I P L E I O V U T C
Z F T S A N C T I F I C A T I O N H Y W
L Y J B O Z B H I G H W A Y D H J D N M
```

OUTSIDE THE CAMP	BEARING HIS CROSS	WORLD'S SIN	INDIVIDUAL
DISCIPLE	MASTER	TESTIMONY	CONFORMITY
OVERFLOWING	AFFECTION	SEPARATION	GO FORTH
WITNESS-BEARER	STRAIGHT AND NARROW	LIONLIKE	SANCTIFICATION
HIGHWAY	HOLINESS	COMMUNION	CROWN OF GLORY

Morning

In the name of the LORD I will destroy them.
—Psalm 118:12

Our Lord Jesus, by His death, did not purchase a right to only a part of us, but to our entire being. In His crucifixion and death, He contemplated our entire sanctification—spirit, soul, and body—so that in this triple kingdom, He Himself might reign supreme without a rival. It is the business of the newborn nature that God has given to the regenerated to assert the rights of the Lord Jesus Christ. My soul, since you are a child of God, you must conquer each part of yourself that is not submitted to Christ; you must surrender all your powers and passions to the silver scepter of Jesus' gracious reign. You must never be satisfied until He who is King by purchase becomes King by gracious coronation and reigns supreme in your life. Seeing then that sin has no right to any part of us, we go about a good and lawful warfare when we seek, in the name of God, to drive it out. My body, you are a member of Christ. Will you tolerate your subjection to the prince of darkness? My soul, Christ has suffered for your sins and redeemed you with His most precious blood. Will you permit your memory to become a storehouse of evil or your passions to be firebrands of iniquity? Will you surrender your judgment to be perverted by error or your will to be chained by sin? No, my soul, you are Christ's, and sin has no right to you. Be courageous concerning this, Christian! Do not be discouraged as though your spiritual enemies could never be destroyed. You are able to overcome them, though not in your own strength; the weakest of them would be too much for you in that. But you can and will overcome them through the blood of the Lamb. Do not ask, "How will I banish them, for they are greater and mightier than I?" but go to the strong for strength, wait humbly on God, and the mighty God of Jacob will surely come to your rescue. Then you will sing of victory through His grace.

```
C E P H S F V W N E W B O R N K C A H A
O W N Q M V J O M L C H J H L Z X L U P
N T D T Y C O N T E M P L A T E D J D X
Q S D U I W Q U P H F R Z P L N O S Z I
U F F J Z R L X J E Y E N F S U O I N S
E Q D W Z R E I G N J G R A Z Z F L A A
R C T E S A Y B Q N U A Z L F Z Z V M N
T O I O S U Z C E V I C T O R Y H E E C
K R J V T T P B A I F M H W P A B R O T
B O L J H P R R R H N D T F E B H S F I
Z N P N B I X O E M F G D I K M C C T F
R A O Y G B X R Y M V W D O N Y U E H I
N T N M C R E G E N E R A T E D B P E C
U I I C R U C I F I X I O N C M E T L A
D O Y R P X S J H V M Q J Y B Y I E O T
M N W I T H O U T R I V A L T K A R R I
G S A A G S U R R E N D E R U X J I D O
N A T U R E M R E S C U E S W C K N M N
V B S H P E P U R C H A S E F O B D Y J
T U W U T R I P L E K I N G D O M M Q Z
```

NAME OF THE LORD	DESTROY	PURCHASE	ENTIRE BEING
CRUCIFIXION	CONTEMPLATED	SANCTIFICATION	TRIPLE KINGDOM
REIGN	SUPREME	WITHOUT RIVAL	NEWBORN
CONQUER	REGENERATED	SURRENDER	SILVER SCEPTER
CORONATION	NATURE	RESCUE	VICTORY

I am poured out like water, and all my bones are out of joint.
—Psalm 22:14

Did earth or heaven ever behold a sadder spectacle of woe? In soul and body, our Lord felt Himself to be weak as water poured on the ground. The placing of the cross in its socket had shaken Him with great violence, had strained all the ligaments, pained every nerve, and more or less dislocated all His bones. Burdened with His own weight, the majestic Sufferer felt the strain increasing every moment of those six long hours. His sense of faintness and general weakness were overpowering, while to His own consciousness He became nothing but a mass of misery and swooning sickness. When Daniel saw the great vision, he thus described his sensations, *"There remained no strength in me: for my comeliness was turned in me into corruption, and I retained no strength"* (Dan. 10:8). How much more faint must have been our greater Prophet when He saw the dread vision of the wrath of God and felt it in His own soul! To us, sensations such as our Lord endured would have been unbearable, and kind unconsciousness would have come to our rescue; but in His case, He was wounded and felt the sword; He drained the cup and tasted every drop.

O King of Grief! (a title strange, yet true
　　To Thee of all kings only due,)
O King of Wounds! how shall I grieve for Thee,
　　Who in all grief preventest me!

As we kneel before our now ascended Savior's throne, let us remember well the way by which He prepared it as a throne of grace for us. Let us in spirit drink of His cup, so that we may be strengthened for our hour of heaviness whenever it may come. In His natural body every member suffered, and so must it be in the spiritual. But as out of all His grief and woes His body came forth uninjured to glory and power, even so will His spiritual body come through the furnace with not so much as the smell of fire on it.

```
D F K F E V E R Y D R O P B M L K E Q V
P O U R E D O U T V E M U J Y H N H P I
L D Z F V U P Z F K R G R Y O F E Q B O
Q B G F P C U V P Z N U Q C U P E S P L
E Y O T U V P S T Y B V L L N B L T K E
L X B E Q R T I A M K Y E E I U T R I N
Z J E F N R L N H Y I T P A X N R I E V C
W G W B W O M A R O N R C K J D K N J E
B B M Y H I V N C O P Q O I U E G G I U
X K G V V D C L G E N D M N R N F T D P
S O U L A N D B O D Y E V G E E E H A R
P G W R A T H O F G O D O O D D W E N E
R E S H H J V K A G M M E F W U H N I P
O P D E T N K Q I D Y I I G G K P F E A
P X X E W S U F F E R E R R R R R D Q L R
H J F P Q J Z H X H A I C I L L A Q K E
E G J N L S F V O C H G L E F G I C X D
T D R A N K T H E C U P J F I S K O E M
Y B Y R P S T U N B E A R A B L E C W G
S P E C T A C L E R M A J E S T I C D D
```

POURED OUT	SPECTACLE	SOUL AND BODY	VIOLENCE
BURDENED	MAJESTIC	SUFFERER	DANIEL
PROPHET	WRATH OF GOD	UNBEARABLE	DRANK THE CUP
EVERY DROP	KING OF GRIEF	KNEEL	PREPARED
THRONE OF GRACE	STRENGTHEN	UNINJURED	FURNACE

Morning

Look upon mine affliction and my pain; and forgive all my sins.
—Psalm 25:18

It is well for us when prayers about our sorrows are linked with pleas concerning our sins—when, being under God's hand, we are not wholly absorbed with our pain, but remember our offenses against God. It is well, also, to take both sorrow and sin to the same place. It was to God that David carried his sorrow, and it was to God that David confessed his sin. Notice that we must take our sorrows to God. You may give even your little sorrows to God, for He counts the hairs of your head; your great sorrows you may commit to Him, for He holds the ocean in the hollow of His hand. Go to Him, whatever your present trouble may be, and you will find Him willing and able to relieve you. But we must take our sins to God, too. We must carry them to the cross so that the blood may fall upon them, to purge away their guilt and to destroy their defiling power. The special lesson of the text is this: in the right spirit, we are to go to the Lord with our sorrows and our sins. Note that all David asked concerning his sorrow was, *"Look upon mine affliction and my pain."* But the next petition is vastly more precise, definite, decided, plain: *"Forgive all my sins."* Many sufferers would have put it, "Remove my affliction and my pain, and look at my sins." But David did not say this. He cried, "Lord, as for my affliction and my pain, I will not dictate to Your wisdom. Lord, look at them. I will leave them to You. I would be glad to have my pain removed, but do as You desire. But as for my sins, Lord, I know what I want to happen to them. I must have them forgiven; I cannot endure to lie under their curse for a moment longer." A Christian considers sorrow to be lighter on the scale than sin; he can bear it if his troubles continue, but he cannot support the burden of his transgressions.

```
R I E T L J B V R E L I E V E T J Y M C
Y F Z R I D C R G O C W E V E V X A P R
A T Z O G R F C P T X N W K T O Y U R O
X F L U H S O R R O W S V R J W O O B S
G Q Q B T W D G J Q G X Q B D N F M H S
U K J L E Z I B B A V K L T U W F G O K
R Z C E R P P O X V C X G I E T E A L C
W I H A D H B K C K K M S A D Q N N L C
O U B D A V I D G E X I Y V P S S Y O O
Q V I I A V X L T U A W F S I J E B W N
D J S P R A Y E R S B N O F I B S F D F
W H I F K M V M V X A N R N O N R U X E
M H R B E O W O A W W X G S B O S P X S
A F F L I C T I O N N N I P C J U R N S
G S V A B O U R P A I N V A F A X M T I
G C A R R I E D M W T H E W Z E L Y W O
T J L N Q G B M H B I Z K V H S J E R N
O W D L K P E T I T I O N S M T Y H X A
Z Z V P R E S E N T J U R P J V Z Q A Y
R D Q B U R D E N S Q N I E W M I D G F
```

AFFLICTION	SORROWS	FORGIVE	PRAYERS
OFFENSES	DAVID	CARRIED	TROUBLE
OCEAN	HOLLOW	RELIEVE	CROSS
PETITIONS	LIGHTER	SCALE	BURDENS
MY SINS	OUR PAIN	CONFESSION	PRESENT

My God, my God, why hast thou forsaken me?
—Psalm 22:1

We here behold the Savior in the depth of His sorrows. No other place so well shows the grief of Christ as Calvary, and no other moment at Calvary is so full of agony as that in which His cry rends the air—*"My God, my God, why hast thou forsaken me?"* At this moment physical weakness was united with acute mental torture from the shame and ignominy through which He had to pass. He suffered spiritual agony surpassing all expression, resulting from the departure of His Father's presence, unbearably heightening His grief. This was the black midnight of His horror. It was then that He descended into the abyss of suffering. No man can enter into the full meaning of these words. Some of us think at times that we could cry, "My God, my God, why have You forsaken me?" There are seasons when the brightness of our Father's smile is eclipsed by clouds and darkness, but let us remember that God never really forsakes us. It is only an illusory forsaking with us, but in Christ's case, it was a real forsaking. We grieve at a little withdrawal of our Father's love; but the real turning away of God's face from His Son, who will calculate how deep the agony that it caused Him? In our case, our cry is often dictated by unbelief. In His case, it was the utterance of a dreadful fact, for God had really turned away from Him for a season. O poor, distressed soul, who once lived in the sunshine of God's face, but are now in darkness, remember that He has not really forsaken you. God in the clouds is as much our God as when He shines forth in all the luster of His grace. But since even the thought that He has forsaken us gives us agony, what must the woe of the Savior have been when He exclaimed, *"My God, my God, why hast thou forsaken me?"*

```
V D E G L S I W U X F G D P M Y G O D K
I G L L I U Y W U R V H P R E H U L T I
T V U X L N W H D K A X B E Y L L S N B
F E S Z H S Q I V P G K T S V C U H N N
O X T I Z H Q I T Z J Q B E R Q I I Y F
R C E L B I T O D H Z M P N E K G N N Q
S L R D W N O S U H D L X C G P N E D I
A A K D X E Q Q P R X R X E F Y O S D S
K I C A L V A R Y O B N A E T F M Z E P
E M D S A W O X W G L V S W R O I U P H
N E C L I P S E D E W G C H A W N H A Y
R D B H T X S U X D F S A O A L Y G R S
V Y G J T S D A H A T E Y A W M A I T I
F T E Y Z Z T G Z G E A V K Q K E A U C
S F T Y O C M O P L V S M O M F G O R A
C O C B Y X F N K O S O W K Q Q R P E L
V J Z H K S Y V X W N Q U T L I J C N
G Z B W E A K N E S S P Z O T B E B X P
W L F N X J C Z H S Z M D A E V F L V T
Y C L O U D S W M I D N I G H T O S V Y
```

MY GOD	FORSAKEN	CALVARY	AGONY
PHYSICAL	WEAKNESS	SHAME	IGNOMINY
DEPARTURE	PRESENCE	GRIEF	MIDNIGHT
ECLIPSED	WITHDRAWAL	SUNSHINE	CLOUDS
SHINES	LUSTER	SEASON	EXCLAIMED

Morning

Lift them up for ever.
—Psalm 28:9

God's people need lifting up. They are very heavy by nature. They have no wings, or, if they have, they are like the dove of old that lay among the pots; and they need divine grace to make them mount on wings covered with silver and feathers of yellow gold. By nature *"sparks fly upward"* (Job 5:7), but the sinful souls of men fall downward. O Lord, *"lift them up for ever"*! David himself said, *"Unto thee, O Lord, do I lift up my soul"* (Ps. 25:1), and he here felt the necessity that other men's souls should be lifted up as well as his own. When you ask this blessing for yourself, do not forget to seek it for others. There are three ways in which God's people need to be lifted up. They need to be elevated in character. Lift them up, O Lord; do not permit Your people to be like the world's people. The world lies in the wicked one; lift them out of it. The world's people are looking after silver and gold, seeking their own pleasures and the gratification of their lusts; but, Lord, lift Your people up above all this. Keep them from being "muckrakers," as John Bunyan called the man who was always scraping after gold. Set their hearts upon their risen Lord and their heavenly heritage. Moreover, believers need to be prospered in conflict. In battle, if they seem to fall, O Lord, be pleased to give them the victory. If the enemy's foot is upon their necks for a moment, help them to grasp the sword of the Spirit and eventually win the battle. Lord, lift up Your children's spirits in the day of conflict. Do not let them sit in the dust, mourning forever. Do not allow the adversary to vex them sorely and make them fret. But if they have been persecuted like Hannah (see 1 Samuel 1:2–20), let them sing of the mercy of a delivering God. We may also ask our Lord to lift them up on the Last Day. Lift them up by taking them home, lift their bodies from the tomb, and raise their souls to Your eternal kingdom in glory.

```
U I A Y H E R I T A G E J H C E V B C O
Y X B O C I R W Z O R M D L Z L B I H C
Z W L P R O S P E R E D C N V E F D A O
G L E B Y E L L O W G O L D Q V J O R N
S I S T Z V J I N T X T V X J A O V A F
N F S A B O S E R I R S P X X T J E C L
O T I A D E L I V E R A N C E E F K T I
A U N X F O R E V E R W N N W D N E E C
G P G O R D Q R Q H F F L R J P H X R T
Q D O T M H Z I P G L M X B J R K U M W
H Q S J I Z R V J Z P W O H B U E E X R
E X I W W N Q F K B X Y H U M M V E M R
A P L M E R C Y A R E X U E N K R E S O
V S V K T C B R G N B D D G A T J K T V
Y Z E T E R N A L K I N G D O M S P J Y
C G R D C Q M V I C Y R I U I J R I B Q
G Q J D Q R C T N O J U H M F P V S Q Y
Z B B Y X R I F L A S T D A Y D G D F P
H Q R I S E N L O R D A R X V O J I G Z
G J V I C T O R Y W I N G S G N S L I W
```

LIFT UP	FOREVER	HEAVY	WINGS
DOVE	MOUNT	SILVER	YELLOW GOLD
BLESSING	ELEVATED	CHARACTER	RISEN LORD
HERITAGE	PROSPERED	CONFLICT	VICTORY
MERCY	DELIVERANCE	LAST DAY	ETERNAL KINGDOM

109

Evening

Rise up, my love, my fair one, and come away.
—Song of Solomon 2:10

I hear the voice of my Beloved! He speaks to me. Fair weather is smiling upon the face of the earth, and He would not have me spiritually asleep while nature is all around me awaking from her winter's rest. He bids me, *"Rise up,"* and well He may, for I have long enough been lying among the campfires of worldliness. He is risen, and I am risen in Him. Why then should I cleave to the dust? From lower loves, desires, pursuits, and aspirations, I would rise toward Him. He calls me by the sweet title of *"My love,"* and counts me fair; this is a good argument for my rising. If He has exalted me and thinks I am beautiful, how can I linger in the tents of Kedar and find congenial associates among the sons of men? He bids me, *"Come away."* Further and further from everything selfish, groveling, worldly, sinful, He calls me; yes, from the outwardly religious world that does not know Him and has no sympathy with the mystery of the higher life, He calls me. *"Come away"* has no harsh sound in it to my ear, for what is there to hold me in this wilderness of vanity and sin? O my Lord, if only I could come away, but I am taken among the thorns and cannot escape from them as I want to. I would, if it were possible, have neither eyes, nor ears, nor heart for sin. You call me to Yourself by saying, *"Come away,"* and this is a melodious call indeed. To come to You is to come home from exile, to come to land out of the raging storm, to come to rest after long labor, to come to the goal of my desires and the summit of my wishes. But Lord, how can a stone rise, or how can a lump of clay come away from the horrible pit? Oh, raise me; draw me. Your grace can do it. Send forth Your Holy Spirit to kindle sacred flames of love in my heart, and I will continue to rise until I leave life and time behind me, and indeed *"come away."*

```
R  H  W  S  A  S  L  E  E  P  I  N  I  J  E  A  H  T  A  Z
B  R  C  F  B  Z  D  C  W  Q  E  K  T  Z  R  V  P  F  V  C
U  C  C  F  L  M  L  G  G  Y  Z  L  E  M  D  F  N  D  S  F
C  G  W  X  J  A  P  E  N  D  R  D  N  T  P  O  K  N  A  F
J  A  X  R  Q  C  M  F  K  Q  V  X  T  W  U  Y  Y  M  C  O
S  A  M  J  C  O  M  E  A  W  A  Y  S  T  R  X  O  E  R  U
M  I  S  P  K  D  C  A  S  J  E  G  O  G  S  J  V  L  E  C
Y  P  Y  P  F  J  E  A  O  E  N  X  F  Y  U  D  Y  O  D  N
S  Y  F  P  I  I  D  J  D  W  A  I  K  J  I  E  E  D  F  W
T  T  N  U  M  R  R  S  D  Q  B  N  E  B  T  S  W  I  V  E
E  M  T  P  U  E  A  E  M  G  K  B  D  S  G  I  V  O  I  K
R  N  X  W  R  P  W  T  S  Y  P  I  A  E  E  R  U  U  F  L
Y  B  E  U  Q  K  N  V  I  Z  L  P  R  L  R  E  A  S  M  A
N  A  T  U  R  E  Q  N  L  O  A  O  D  F  V  L  I  R  Z  U
Z  U  F  A  I  R  O  N  E  P  N  Q  V  L  J  W  O  I  D  Z
H  G  B  E  A  U  T  I  F  U  L  K  G  E  E  P  V  S  G  D
F  A  I  R  W  E  A  T  H  E  R  E  D  S  M  X  W  E  E  E
U  E  J  A  H  D  F  J  R  P  K  J  A  S  W  R  G  U  C  O
A  W  A  K  E  N  I  N  G  C  Q  A  L  H  A  J  U  P  L  K
W  R  B  J  D  B  E  L  O  V  E  D  F  U  B  B  S  D  E  K
```

RISE UP	FAIR ONE	COME AWAY	BELOVED
FAIR WEATHER	ASLEEP	NATURE	AWAKENING
CAMPFIRES	DESIRE	PURSUIT	ASPIRATION
MY LOVE	BEAUTIFUL	TENTS OF KEDAR	SELFLESS
MYSTERY	MELODIOUS	SACRED	FLAMES

Morning

If any man hear my voice, and open the door, I will come in to him.
—Revelation 3:20

What is your desire this evening? Is it set on heavenly things? Do you long to enjoy the high doctrine of eternal love? Do you desire liberty in very close communion with God? Do you aspire to know the heights, depths, lengths, and breadths of God? Then you must draw near to Jesus. You must get a clear view of Him in His preciousness and completeness. You must see Him in His work, in His offices, and in His person. He who understands Christ receives an anointing from the Holy One, by which He knows all things. Christ is the great master key of all the chambers of God. There is no treasury of God that will not open and yield up all its wealth to the soul that lives near to Jesus. Are you saying, "Oh, that He would dwell in my heart. If only He would make my heart His dwelling place forever"? Open the door, beloved, and He will come into your soul. He has been knocking for a long time, and all with the purpose that He might dine with you and you with Him. He dines with you because you have invited Him into your heart, and you dine with Him because He brings the provision. He could not commune with you if it were not in your heart, you providing the house; and you could not fellowship with Him if He did not bring provision with Him, because you have a bare cupboard. Fling wide, then, the entrance to your soul. He will come with the love that you long to feel. He will come with the joy into which you cannot work your poor depressed spirit. He will bring the peace that now you do not have. He will come with His flagons of wine and sweet apples of love and cheer you until you have no other sickness but that of "love o'erpowering, love divine." Only open the door to Him, drive out His enemies, give Him the keys of your heart, and He will dwell there forever. Oh, wondrous love, that brings such a Guest to dwell in such a heart!

```
D O T U G L O X H H P W L I B E R T Y H
E Q N W S D E P T H S M S V B L L L N E
S T D L D G D G L Z Y W P W E C Q S X A
I O G R V Z I C B I K K M Y V O I C E V
R B F T A J O O U H E A R U M M R H M E
E N A N Y W N X E K R Q C S O P T H O N
M A U U U R N H I Z C F O P B L O Y F L
Y E X A Y M F E Q K V D M R S E H Y J Y
Q B M W N K P Q A C R E E E H T I J Q T
C O M M U N I O N R E F I C V E M B F H
F H E W Y M M F C L H O N I M I Y X H I
P I E T E R N A L L O V E O D Z J A E N
R O B R E A D T H S Q O T U T D G K I G
M O V N L U S R J G G X V S Q D F T G S
H A I R X M K P I K E X W N D H A P H V
X J G M Y G X C Y I O G S X K B N F T K
B J G M O F W D A N O I N T I N G V S I
S Y D L L E N G T H S B J V E D G X X S
H V K C J A Q P G D R G P P E R S O N R
A C T O F F I C E S C Z T W O R K F Z G
```

HEAR	MY VOICE	COME IN	TO HIM
DESIRE	HEAVENLY THINGS	LIBERTY	ETERNAL LOVE
COMMUNION	HEIGHTS	DEPTHS	LENGTHS
BREADTHS	DRAW NEAR	PRECIOUS	COMPLETE
WORK	OFFICES	PERSON	ANOINTING

Evening

How precious also are thy thoughts unto me, O God!
—Psalm 139:17

Divine omniscience affords no comfort to the ungodly mind, but to the child of God it overflows with consolation. God is always thinking about us. He never turns aside His mind from us, and He always has us before His eyes. This is precisely as we would have it, for it would be dreadful to exist for a moment beyond the observation of our heavenly Father. His thoughts are always tender, loving, wise, prudent, and far-reaching. They bring to us countless benefits; therefore, it is a choice delight to remember them. The Lord has always thought about His people: hence, their election and the covenant of grace by which their salvation is secured. He always will think about them: hence, their final perseverance by which they will be brought safely to their final rest. In all our wanderings, the vigilant gaze of the eternal Watcher is always fixed upon us; we never roam beyond the Shepherd's eye. In our sorrows, He observes us incessantly, and not one of our pains escapes His attention. In our toils, He marks all our weariness and writes in His book all the struggles of His faithful ones. These thoughts of the Lord encompass us in all our paths and penetrate the innermost region of our being. Not a nerve or tissue, valve or vessel, of our bodily organization is uncared for; all the details of our little world are thought about by the great God. Dear reader, is this truth precious to you? Then hold to it. Never be led astray by those philosophic fools who preach an impersonal God and talk of self-existent, self-governing matter. The Lord lives and thinks about us; this is a truth far too precious for us to be lightly robbed of it. The notice of a nobleman is valued so highly that he who has it counts his fortune made; but what is it to be thought of by the King of Kings! If the Lord thinks of us, all is well, and we may rejoice forevermore.

```
M B E N E F I T S N U P Z K J H D C N R
H Q Y G A D Q R Q S K E T R I S I O X J
D Z Y D E L I G H T J R T W G L N U Y Z
L E N N X U T J I R N S H E Y J C N W O
E P R E C I O U S U W E O A F H E T A M
Y V W P S Z K C V G V V U R K R S L N N
L O V I N G F H T G H E G I L S S E D I
W H C C Y P F R A L F R H N S H A S E S
P I P R U D E N T E U A T E T R N S R C
A W S P L S J V B S B N S S E I T T I I
S D Z E F Q V P G X B C A S N S L W N E
O B S E R V A T I O N E E M D M Y T G N
J N T V U T J K C I T U N Z I N F D S C
C C M F J S E I I S E V D P N G P D A E
A M E R S D O O W P V W A E G I H G M G
H X X Y P C O N S O L A T I O N X R Z P
O V E R F L O W I N G Q G S L Z V D I B
V F A R R E A C H I N G C O M F O R T B
P U Y L F G P J M R G G S V G I G C U R
W O T N B J G X W Q Y Y U F U Z S J Q F
```

PRECIOUS	THOUGHTS	OMNISCIENCE	COMFORT
CONSOLATION	OVERFLOWING	OBSERVATION	TENDING
LOVING	WISE	PRUDENT	FAR-REACHING
COUNTLESS	BENEFITS	DELIGHT	PERSEVERANCE
WANDERINGS	INCESSANTLY	WEARINESS	STRUGGLES

Morning

His cheeks are as a bed of spices, as sweet flowers.
—Song of Solomon 5:13

The flowery month is here! March winds and April showers have done their work, and the earth is all adorned in beauty. Come, my soul, and put on your holiday attire; go forth to gather garlands of heavenly thoughts. You know where to go, for you know well the *"bed of spices."* You have often smelled the perfume of *"sweet flowers."* You will go at once to your Well Beloved and find all loveliness and all joy in Him. That cheek—once so rudely smitten with a rod, often wet with tears of sympathy and then defiled with spittle—that cheek, as it smiles with mercy, is a fragrant aroma to my heart. You did not hide Your face from shame and spittle, O Lord Jesus; therefore, I will find my dearest delight in praising You. Those cheeks were furrowed by the plow of grief and crimsoned with red lines of blood from Your thorn-crowned temples. Such marks of limitless love cannot but charm my soul far more than great quantities of perfume. If I may not see the whole of His face, I would behold His cheeks, for the least glimpse of Him is exceedingly refreshing to my spiritual sense and yields a variety of delights. In Jesus I find not only fragrance, but *"a bed of spices"*; not one flower, but all manner of *"sweet flowers."* He is to me my Rose and my Lily, my heart's comfort and my healing balm. When He is with me, it is May all year round. My soul goes forth to wash its happy face in the morning dew of His grace and to comfort itself with the singing of the birds of His promises. Precious Lord Jesus, let me truly know the blessedness that dwells in abiding, unbroken fellowship with You. I am a poor worthless one, whose cheek You have deigned to kiss! Oh, let me kiss You in return with the kisses of my lips.

```
R M C H E E K S A L B R T J M G L F K J
R A R S C S F M U I Y L A N Z B U L F K
C C K E G F R Q K M A L L J O Y L O I P
M N D V Y C N C N I M Z A C K L H W F E
C L A D O R N E D T P D U W N I C E L Z
F S Y O I Q A D X L C O W F M P Q R O B
S W E E T B P N G E K P K C E T M P V E
P M R N C X J V Y S K O Z N R H E Z E A
E D P C A Y Q K Z S D S V T Z O R L L U
R V E P W E L L B E L O V E D L C Z I T
F C Q R R F R X N H O M F M S I Y S N Y
U F Y I D C C U F L A I R I A D G Y E R
M B V Q P V Z J Q P E R J F I A L M S K
E K U V Q H X F Y E Q F O G Q Y F P S V
B E D O F S P I C E S B B M S E L A N P
I G A R L A N D S R F F P S A K H T Y Q
V F Z R O S E A N D L I L Y H Z F H L Z
W U W U B K F Q U A N T I T I E S Y S Y
D F G P F R A G R A N T B K X Y S X P O
I M M Q M D H E A V E N L Y U V H G E Q
```

CHEEKS	BED OF SPICES	SWEET	FLOWER
ADORNED	BEAUTY	HOLIDAY	GARLANDS
HEAVENLY	PERFUME	WELL BELOVED	LOVELINESS
ALL JOY	SYMPATHY	MERCY	FRAGRANT
AROMA	LIMITLESS	QUANTITIES	ROSE AND LILY

Evening

A very present help.
—Psalm 46:1

Covenant blessings are not meant to be only looked at; they are intended to be appropriated. Even our Lord Jesus is given to us for our present use. Believer, do you make use of Christ as you should? When you are in trouble, why do you not tell Him all your grief? Does He not have a sympathizing heart, and can He not comfort and relieve you? No, you are going about to all your friends, except for your best Friend, and you are telling your tale everywhere except to the heart of your Lord. Are you burdened with this day's sins? Here is a fountain filled with blood: use it, saint; use it. Has a sense of guilt returned to you? The pardoning grace of Jesus may be proved again and again. Come to Him at once for cleansing. Do you deplore your weakness? He is your strength; why not lean on Him? Do you feel naked? Come here, soul; put on the robe of Jesus' righteousness. Do not stand looking at it, but wear it. Strip off your own righteousness and your own fears, too. Put on the fair white linen, for it was meant to wear. Do you feel sick? Pull the night-bell of prayer, and call up the Beloved Physician! He will give the medicine that will revive you. You are poor, but then you have *"a kinsman…, a mighty man of wealth"* (Ruth 2:1). Will you not go to Him and ask Him to give you of His abundance, when He has given you the promise that you will be a joint heir with Him? All that He is and all that He has, He has made available to you. There is nothing Christ dislikes more than for His people to make a display of Him and not to use Him. He loves to be employed by us. The more burdens we put on His shoulders, the more precious He will be to us.

Let us be simple with Him, then,
    Not backward, stiff, or cold,
As though our Bethlehem could be
    What Sinai was of old.

```
T A B U N D A N C E Z V G I G G R L U S
J A H E B Z Q M J Q F K C K J Z I T A V
K S H D E K G S C D Q B R V C E G A V V
I P H Y S I C I A N D Q L Y B Y H X A E
N B X Q T Z O L U E C L Y Q R I T E I N
S Q K M F V B E T H L E H E M O E T L R
M F L M R R K N X E Z V I E Y F O M A W
A E N E I W R M O G J J K M F L U D B P
N J A P E Y G O J T C K Z P E P S Q L R
W K T S N L G P O C T B S L J A N X E E
Q D M D D E L T I O W L T O F R E M P S
F C F P G M Y T N V K E C Y O D S G R E
A P S V W K X X T E Y S L E U O S Y E N
C O M F O R T D H N K S U D N N Q S C T
C P V X H V C A E A S I A K T I W A I H
P X X K T F C O I N Z N H H A N G I O E
A G U Y Z S D V R T W G O E I G C N U L
N R E L I E V E L U J S R V N S P T S P
T X X Q T O Q B U R D E N E D U K M A Q
J V W Y S D Y A P P R O P R I A T E D C
```

PRESENT HELP	COVENANT	BLESSINGS	APPROPRIATED
COMFORT	RELIEVE	BEST FRIEND	BURDENED
FOUNTAIN	SAINT	PARDONING	RIGHTEOUSNESS
PHYSICIAN	KINSMAN	ABUNDANCE	JOINT HEIR
AVAILABLE	EMPLOYED	PRECIOUS	BETHLEHEM

Morning

Great multitudes followed him, and he healed them all.
—Matthew 12:15

What an abundance of hideous sickness must have thrust itself under the eye of Jesus! Yet we do not read that He was disgusted by it; instead, He patiently waited on every case. What an unusual variety of evils must have met at His feet! What sickening ulcers and putrefying sores! Yet He was ready for every new shape of monstrous evil, and He was victor over it in every form. Let the arrow fly from what quarter it might; He quenched its fiery power. The heat of fever or the cold of dropsy; the lethargy of palsy or the rage of madness; the filth of leprosy or the darkness of blindness—all knew the power of His word and fled at His command. In every corner of the field He was triumphant over evil and received the respect of delivered captives. He came, He saw, He conquered everywhere. It is even so this morning. Whatever my own case may be, the beloved Physician can heal me. Whatever may be the state of others whom I may remember at this moment in prayer, I may have hope in Jesus that He will be able to heal them of their sins. My child, my friend, my dearest one, I can have hope for each, for all, when I remember the healing power of my Lord. On my own account, however severe my struggle with sins and infirmities, I may yet be of good cheer. He who walked on earth healing the sick still dispenses His grace and works wonders among the sons of men. Let me go to Him at once in earnest. Let me praise Him this morning, as I remember how He performed His spiritual cures, which bring Him most renown. It was by taking our sicknesses on Himself. *"With his stripes we are healed"* (Isa. 53:5). The church on earth is full of souls healed by our beloved Physician. The inhabitants of heaven itself confess that He healed them all. Come, then, my soul; tell about the virtue of His grace everywhere, and let it be *to the Lord for a name, for an everlasting sign that shall not be cut off"* (Isa. 55:13).

```
U  Z  P  A  T  I  E  N  T  L  Y  S  D  V  Q  T  W  B  G  D
P  H  M  E  A  Q  U  X  N  X  Q  C  W  H  H  F  O  H  E  Z
I  C  R  U  N  C  U  R  E  S  I  H  W  S  C  P  R  F  P  X
J  L  A  I  L  S  X  G  K  O  K  R  X  B  M  E  K  H  K  M
E  N  R  P  Q  T  A  K  U  B  X  M  H  F  S  R  W  E  T  J
P  N  A  E  T  S  I  F  M  D  T  X  M  B  I  F  O  A  R  F
Y  S  Y  B  T  I  Y  T  A  P  F  F  T  Q  C  O  N  L  I  E
N  Z  T  P  R  G  V  J  U  O  P  W  M  J  K  R  D  E  U  E
B  L  Q  I  W  N  M  E  F  D  T  T  V  K  N  M  E  D  M  Y
V  A  Z  T  C  V  S  G  S  R  E  K  S  Y  E  E  R  O  P  E
C  I  B  Y  H  O  B  V  V  F  U  S  C  L  S  D  S  B  H  O
G  L  C  P  R  Y  M  H  I  S  W  O  R  D  S  W  R  M  A  F
R  V  W  T  R  Q  Q  M  S  R  L  U  W  P  Z  Q  H  W  N  J
N  H  U  N  O  E  Q  K  A  F  T  O  M  K  R  T  X  H  T  E
S  K  G  P  A  R  N  I  S  N  L  U  Q  B  F  E  F  S  P  S
L  D  D  E  L  I  V  E  R  E  D  H  E  Y  G  T  A  E  T  U
K  U  H  O  K  H  W  K  Q  P  K  V  R  V  R  B  F  D  N  S
H  P  W  A  I  T  I  N  G  C  P  Z  Y  O  L  N  C  O  Y  K
H  C  M  L  K  U  I  Y  A  S  T  P  O  W  E  R  C  F  H  D
O  E  V  E  V  E  R  L  A  S  T  I  N  G  X  N  Z  F  K  M
```

MULTITUDES	HEALED	SICKNESS	EYE OF JESUS
PATIENTLY	WAITING	READY	VICTOR
POWER	HIS WORD	COMMAND	TRIUMPHANT
DELIVERED	CAPTIVES	WORK WONDERS	PERFORMED
CURES	VIRTUE	EVERLASTING	SIGN

DAY 30

Evening

Jesus saith unto him, Rise, take up thy bed, and walk.
—John 5:8

Like many others, the crippled man had been waiting for a miracle to happen and for a sign to be given. Wearily, he watched the pool, but no angel came or came for him; yet, thinking it was his only chance, he waited still. He did not know that there was One near him whose word could heal him in a moment. Many are in the same plight. They are waiting for some extraordinary emotion, remarkable impression, or heavenly vision. They wait in vain and watch for nothing. Even supposing that, in a few cases, remarkable signs are seen, yet these are rare, and no one has a right to look for them in his own situation— especially no one who feels his inability to avail himself of the moving of the water even if it did come. It is very sad to realize that tens of thousands are now waiting on the use of means, ordinances, vows, or resolutions, and they have waited in vain, utterly in vain, longer than one can imagine. Meanwhile these poor souls forget the present Savior, who invites them to look to Him and be saved. He could heal them immediately, but they prefer to wait for an angel or a miracle. To trust God is the sure way to every blessing, and He is worthy of the most implicit confidence; but unbelief makes them prefer the cold porches of Bethesda to the warm bosom of His love. Oh, that the Lord may turn His eye upon the multitudes who are in this situation tonight. May He forgive the slights that they put upon His divine power. In His sweet, constraining voice, may He call them to rise from their beds of despair and in the energy of faith to take up their beds and walk. O Lord, hear our prayers for everyone who is in this situation tonight. At this calm hour of sunset and before the day breaks, may they look and live. Dear reader, is there anything in this passage that speaks to you?

```
E W E X T R A O R D I N A R Y D E T V E
A A G M U O O C C Q R N S C K M X T D A
S L Y O M A Q H B D X L N I D P K R Y V
I K I V I F T M R D Y X Z N G B R E L A
G Q K I N K Q J E R F K T R E N G S D I
N W D N O S E Z M J C B K N C M S O J L
Z X M G Z P M U A F X Y B A Y I E L L X
T M A W P O O C R O V P W I C R L U V X
Q L W A H O T E K S S U Y M I A K T S F
J J S T E L I V A R K U C A S C R I Y O
M W H E A K O I B F S M I G P L D O K R
W D U R V Y N S L W C Z C I L E C N C D
C Q X V E R C I E W R C U N I X D S M I
C Q C R N S X O J I M P R E S S I O N N
B H P A L D P N V P V U O U A Z F I C A
O R H O Y N B H M L M T H O R B M H K N
S G T E M S I T U A T I O N V P R D J C
J K U W I N V I T E S G I V E C T E G E
R W A S Q H J R F L I G H T A N G E L S
I H J P Q J Y I G X E P R X Y C C A N J
```

MIRACLE	A SIGN	POOL	ANGEL
FLIGHT	EXTRAORDINARY	EMOTION	REMARKABLE
IMPRESSION	HEAVENLY	VISION	SIGNS
SITUATION	AVAIL	MOVING WATER	ORDINANCES
RESOLUTIONS	IMAGINE	INVITES	WALK

Morning

He that was healed wist not who it was.
—John 5:13

Years are short to the happy and healthy, but thirty-eight years of disease must have dragged into a long time for the poor, impotent man. When Jesus, therefore, healed him by a word, while he lay at the pool of Bethesda, he was delightfully aware of a change. Likewise, the sinner who has for weeks and months been paralyzed with despair, and has wearily sighed for salvation, is very conscious of the change when the Lord Jesus speaks the word of power and gives joy and peace in believing. The evil removed is too great to be removed without our discerning it, the life imparted is too remarkable to be possessed and remain inoperative, and the change is too marvelous not to be perceived. Yet the poor man was ignorant of the Author of his cure. He did not know the sacredness of His person, the offices that He sustained, or the mission that brought Him among men. Much ignorance of Jesus may remain in hearts that yet feel the power of His blood. We must not hastily condemn men for lack of knowledge; but where we can see the faith that saves the soul, we must believe that salvation has been bestowed. The Holy Spirit makes men penitents long before He makes them holy. He who believes what he knows will soon know more clearly what he believes. Ignorance is, however, an evil, for this poor man was much tantalized by the Pharisees and was quite unable to cope with them. It is good to be able to answer the opposition, but we cannot do so if we do not know the Lord Jesus clearly and with understanding. The cure of his ignorance, however, soon followed the cure of his infirmity, for he was visited by the Lord in the temple. After that gracious manifestation, he was found testifying that *"it was Jesus, which had made him whole"* (John 5:15). Lord, if You have saved me, show me Yourself, so that I may declare You to the sons of men.

```
T C O N S C I O U S W X A C I Q B M P G
Q D R W O R D O F P O W E R O Q E K Z H
J I E P D W P J D V N S H O S V T L B A
V S M H Q E W N W U L A Y D Z D H G R X
B E O J A Y S D Q V Z L H O V J E C J M
B A V F P P T P J S M V Q E D H S J H A
K S E O P E P L A E P A P J A S D N D R
G E D W E K R Y N I U T R F T L A N Q V
S Z U X N O H C J L R I S W D E T D M E
W R N F I R W U E F M O A M D Z I H A L
W I R Z T P M H Y I N N S W W F K K Y O
Y X U D E R B I I U V N A J A Z J S H U
H M V K N N W A X F D E B P Y R U A C S
G F T D T I P D P O O T D C R P E C H H
C L I A I Q B E L I E V I N G B I R A T
L K L D J L G O R J G S J H M Z F E N Q
L I F E I M P A R T E D P W W T G D G X
D E L I G H T F U L S F Q F V M U X E Q
M M E J O Y A N D P E A C E I G K H J D
O S I P A R A L Y Z E D W B F T A G B I
```

HAPPY	HEALTHY	DISEASE	BETHESDA
DELIGHTFUL	AWARE	CHANGE	PARALYZED
DESPAIR	SALVATION	CONSCIOUS	WORD OF POWER
JOY AND PEACE	BELIEVING	REMOVED	LIFE IMPARTED
MARVELOUS	PERCEIVED	SACRED	PENITENT

125

Acquaint now thyself with him.
—Job 22:21

If we desire to properly acquaint ourselves with God and be at peace, we must know Him as He has revealed Himself—not only in the unity of His essence and existence, but also in the plurality of His persons. *"God said, Let us make man in our image"* (Gen. 1:26). Do not let man be content until he knows something of the *"us"* from whom his being was derived. Endeavor to know the Father; bury your head in His bosom in deep repentance, and confess that you are not worthy to be called His child. Receive the kiss of His love. Let the ring that is the token of His eternal faithfulness be on your finger. Sit at His table, and let your heart be made merry in His grace. Then press forward and seek to know much of the Son of God, who is the brightness of His Father's glory; yet, in unspeakable condescension of grace, He became Man for our sakes. Know Him in the unique complexity of His nature: eternal God, yet suffering, finite man. Follow Him as He walks the waters with the footsteps of deity and as He sits on the well in the weariness of humanity. Do not be satisfied unless you know much of Jesus Christ as your Friend, your Brother, your Husband, your All. Do not forget the Holy Spirit. Endeavor to obtain a clear view of His nature and character, His attributes, and His works. Behold that Spirit of the Lord, who first of all moved upon chaos and brought forth order; who now visits the chaos of your soul and creates the order of holiness. Behold Him as the Lord and Giver of spiritual life, the Illuminator, the Instructor, the Comforter, and the Sanctifier. Behold Him as, in holy power, He descends on the head of Jesus, and then afterward rests on you who are as the skirts of His garments. Such an intelligent, scriptural, and experiential belief in the Trinity in Unity is yours if you truly know God. Such knowledge brings peace indeed!

```
E C U B M S I W G P E S S E N C E A E S
E O C O N T E N T G U Y L J L G W H X H
Z N D X O K B F Y N L P J F C A K F I H
S D V E E G Q F R N W O R O N R I P S A
Z E V V R T B R B M G U K O G Z O N T C
T S I C F I E X R C M R O T I C H W E Q
K C F C I A V R R V R I M S N Y W I N U
O E N T A Z I E N I J M B T M I O S C A
S N L I B T A T D A H A A E E G S A E I
B S J B W D P C H F L G P P M H H T C N
C I H R O U F E Y F Y E O S Z B Q I M T
S O P E K G F H A H U M A N I T Y S C J
I N X Z L I Q Z V C J L S O I P Z F H Z
C G Z A G Z Q Y K D E M N R C C I I H V
K L U N I T Y L F L G L D E N V P E B O
F S Y N M I E N D E A V O R S W K D I R
Q U U N S P E A K A B L E X Z S B X W D
P L U R A L I T Y Y Y M R V Y B H B E E
G V Z C H A O S D G P H B M M W Q G X R
O J P R E V E A L E D S K T S I U E P V
```

ACQUAINT	AT PEACE	REVEALED	UNITY
ESSENCE	EXISTENCE	PLURALITY	OUR IMAGE
CONTENT	DERIVED	ENDEAVOR	ETERNAL
FAITHFULNESS	UNSPEAKABLE	CONDESCENSION	FOOTSTEPS
HUMANITY	SATISFIED	CHAOS	ORDER

Morning

But now is Christ risen from the dead.
—1 Corinthians 15:20

The whole system of Christianity rests on the fact that Christ is risen from the dead, for *"If Christ be not risen, then is our preaching vain, and your faith is also vain....Ye are yet in your sins"* (1 Cor. 15:14, 17). The divinity of Christ finds its surest proof in His resurrection, since He was *"declared to be the Son of God with power, according to the spirit of holiness, by the resurrection from the dead"* (Rom. 1:4). It would not be unreasonable to doubt His deity if He had not risen. Moreover, Christ's sovereignty depends on His resurrection, *"For to this end Christ both died, and rose, and revived, that he might be Lord both of the dead and living"* (Rom. 14:9). Again, our justification, that choice blessing of the covenant, is linked with Christ's triumphant victory over death and the grave; for He *"was delivered for our offences, and was raised again for our justification"* (Rom. 4:25). Moreover, our very regeneration is connected with His resurrection, for we are *"begotten...again unto a lively hope by the resurrection of Jesus Christ from the dead"* (1 Pet. 1:3). And most certainly our ultimate resurrection rests here, for *"if the Spirit of him that raised up Jesus from the dead dwell in you, he that raised up Christ from the dead shall also quicken your mortal bodies by his Spirit that dwelleth in you"* (Rom. 8:11). If Christ is not risen, then we will not rise; but if He is risen, then they who are asleep in Christ have not perished, but in their flesh will surely behold their God. Thus, the silver thread of resurrection runs through all the believer's blessings, from his regeneration to his eternal glory, and it binds them together. How important, then, will this glorious fact be in his estimation, and how will he rejoice that beyond a doubt it is established that *"now is Christ risen from the dead."*

The promise is fulfill'd,
   Redemption's work is done,
Justice with mercy's reconciled,
   For God has raised His Son.

```
V S P I R I T O F H O L I N E S S V F T
K D A R S V M I D I V I N I T Y P U W S
C C H R I S T J X J T D B R J A R M F O
F M W F T R D E C L A R E D V C E J I N
L C W N Z R F G X R C G V I D H A I F O
B H W C Y I H I M Z O C M E S X C D R F
H R C M A N I F E S T A T I O N H N E G
W I M T P E N I T E N T L O Z U I A S O
G S T S G A A A L Y G C F S N W N M U D
R T W E H A R Y Z T Z X Q A M A G B R N
A I H Q T X I E H D P N Y V I N P S R C
C A S O V E R E I G N T Y D O T Y Q E A
I N X I E R A Q T W P B T E O T H U C K
O I J O T H Q W J Q N Q R I X C M I T M
U T P W T S V Y N X R W V T N F Q C I O
S Y O O V F F S U G P S A Y B J X K O X
I H W D Z A V G T M M O I Z V M K E N H
L R E C Y T L L C P C F N C M I Y N B Y
A N R J V I C T O R Y R I S E N Q N B S
Q N Y T R I U M P H A N T T P T R H J K
```

CHRIST	RISEN	CHRISTIANITY	PREACHING
VAIN	FAITH	DIVINITY	DECLARED
SON OF GOD	POWER	SPIRIT OF HOLINESS	RESURRECTION
DEITY	SOVEREIGNTY	TRIUMPHANT	VICTORY
QUICKEN	PENITENT	MANIFESTATION	GRACIOUS

Evening

★ ★ ★ ★ ★

The only begotten of the Father, full of grace and truth.
—John 1:14

Believer, you can give your testimony that Christ is the "*only begotten of the Father,*" as well as "*the first begotten of the dead*" (Rev. 1:5). You can say, "He is divine to me, even if He is human to all the world. He has done for me what no one but God could do. He has subdued my stubborn will, melted my hardened heart, opened '*gates of brass, and cut the bars of iron in sunder*' (Ps. 107:16). He has turned my mourning into laughter and my desolation into joy. He has led my captivity captive and made my heart '*rejoice with joy unspeakable and full of glory*' (1 Pet. 1:8). Let others think as they will of Him, to me He must be the '*only begotten of the Father.*'" Blessed be His name! And He is full of grace. Oh, if it had not been for Him, I would never have been saved. He drew me when I struggled to escape from His grace; and, when at last I came to His mercy seat, trembling like a condemned criminal, He said, "Your sins, which are many, are all forgiven: be of good cheer." And He is full of truth. His promises have all been true; not one has failed. I bear witness that no servant ever had such a master as I have. No brother has had a kinsman as He has been to me. No spouse has had a husband as Christ has been to my soul. No sinner has had a better Savior; no mourner has had a better comforter than Christ has been to my spirit. I desire no one besides Him. In life, He is my life; in death, He will be the death of death. In poverty, Christ is my riches; in sickness, He makes my bed. In darkness, He is my star; in brightness, He is my sun. He is the manna of the camp in the wilderness, and He will be the new corn of the host when they come to Canaan. Jesus is all grace and no wrath to me, all truth and no falsehood. He is full of truth and grace, infinitely full. My soul, this night, with all your strength, bless "*the only begotten.*"

```
Y Q D E I H K I A N J L W C F B U W W V
W M Z A X G T R Z T A F R L O E O S K S
O L W B Z J R I G U P S J T R H N S M K
E Z R F O F O K F C R T R E G S L G J D
E B M D P D A Y M A Y U P M I W Y R K I
D J K C H Y Q M Q P M B J N V L B A R V
H G I D K I N S M A N B L F E N E C M I
D A A P E R I C M Y Q O G L N G G E E N
X L R M Y S P O U S E R X R V B O A R E
S V A D O I O V M V G N F D I L T N C P
Q C S U E U Z L R O W X L V X E T D Y B
G D T X G N R H A E A U Z A X S E T S M
E G K B P H E N H T J H O K F S N R E E
Q U I K B P T D I P I O Q I M E H U A L
J J U W P B H E A N A O I G G D V T T T
I H V I H Y U V R U G C N C L F O H G E
G G A T E S O F B R A S S C E O C V Q D
C A P T I V I T Y V T X F G C P Q K V A
S P P Y A K W L J F S U B D U E D F X Z
Z O J D E P R S Y T T E S T I M O N Y N
```

ONLY BEGOTTEN	GRACE AND TRUTH	TESTIMONY	DIVINE
SUBDUED	STUBBORN	HARDENED	MELTED
GATES OF BRASS	MOURNING	LAUGHTER	DESOLATION
JOY	CAPTIVITY	REJOICE	BLESSED
MERCY SEAT	FORGIVEN	KINSMAN	SPOUSE

Morning

So to walk, even as he walked.
—1 John 2:6

Why should Christians imitate Christ? They should do it for their own sakes. If they desire to be in a healthy state of soul, if they want to escape the sickness of sin and enjoy the vigor of growing grace, let Jesus be their model. For the sake of their own happiness, if they would enjoy holy and happy communion with Jesus, and if they would be lifted above the cares and troubles of this world, let them walk even as He walked. There is nothing that can assist you in walking toward heaven with good speed as much as wearing the image of Jesus on your heart to rule all its motions. It is when, by the power of the Holy Spirit, you are enabled to walk with Jesus in His very footsteps that you are happiest and most known to be the sons of God. Peter's position of being *"afar off"* (Luke 22:54) is both unsafe and uneasy. Next, for faith's sake, strive to be like Jesus. Ah, poor faith, you have been sorely shot at by cruel foes, but you have not been wounded half so dangerously by your enemies as by your friends. Who made those wounds in the fair hand of godliness? The one who professed faith but used the dagger of hypocrisy. The man with pretenses who enters the fold, being nothing but a wolf in sheep's clothing, worries the flock more than the lion outside. There is no weapon half so deadly as a Judas-kiss. Inconsistent Christians injure the Gospel more than the sneering critic or the infidel. But, especially for Christ's own sake, imitate His example. Christian, do you love your Savior? Is His name precious to you? Is His cause dear to you? Would you see the kingdoms of the world become His? Is it your desire that He would be glorified? Are you longing that souls should be won to Him? If so, imitate Jesus; be an *"epistle of Christ"* (2 Cor. 3:3), *"known and read of all men"* (v. 2).

```
L  G  Y  N  F  H  K  W  Z  I  C  K  S  C  G  D  M  H  B  P
I  F  O  H  A  P  P  I  N  E  S  S  C  H  O  F  G  P  C  L
F  B  C  O  M  M  U  N  I  O  N  P  F  U  D  K  O  M  S  R
T  U  Z  M  K  H  M  E  R  Y  F  X  H  L  L  Q  F  O  D  O
E  W  V  N  Z  X  O  T  S  M  H  O  E  Z  I  N  T  D  E  G
D  H  O  G  E  C  S  F  T  I  X  K  A  K  N  N  A  E  S  I
A  K  L  E  S  C  V  J  I  Y  P  A  L  Y  E  W  Q  L  I  M
B  Q  O  Z  C  C  N  X  R  H  Z  O  T  P  S  N  X  V  R  I
O  W  P  Q  A  H  E  Z  V  E  O  R  H  E  S  N  J  Y  E  T
V  D  D  R  P  R  F  Q  E  Z  U  W  Y  S  I  Z  K  R  X  A
E  J  E  G  E  I  Q  N  X  C  H  S  I  C  K  N  E  S  S  T
A  F  O  O  T  S  T  E  P  S  A  T  I  V  B  S  K  P  C  E
C  L  B  D  G  T  F  F  F  Y  G  I  Z  R  C  G  P  F  E  H
H  H  A  P  P  Y  X  N  W  O  U  N  D  E  D  K  X  D  J  X
R  L  E  G  O  O  D  S  P  E  E  D  Y  V  T  G  J  J  W  A
I  P  W  S  H  W  H  M  Q  C  J  U  T  Z  I  E  P  Q  R  O
F  G  L  O  R  I  F  I  E  D  W  B  S  P  K  G  L  F  B  K
S  R  E  P  I  S  T  L  E  G  I  S  C  E  Z  V  O  A  X  B
O  W  J  M  I  U  T  W  L  R  D  Y  T  W  I  S  N  R  V  U
G  W  V  Q  M  F  F  R  H  O  L  Y  X  T  X  Z  Y  N  E  K
```

IMITATE	CHRIST	HEALTHY	ESCAPE
SICKNESS	VIGOR	MODEL	HAPPINESS
HOLY	HAPPY	COMMUNION	LIFTED ABOVE
GOOD SPEED	FOOTSTEPS	STRIVE	WOUNDED
GODLINESS	DESIRE	GLORIFIED	EPISTLE

Evening

Thou art my servant; I have chosen thee.
—Isaiah 41:9

If we have received the grace of God in our hearts, its practical effect has been to make us God's servants. We may be unfaithful servants—we certainly are unprofitable ones—yet, blessed be His name, we are His servants, wearing His badge, feeding at His table, and obeying His commands. We were once the servants of sin, but He who made us free has now taken us into His family and taught us obedience to His will. We do not serve our Master perfectly, but we would if we could. As we hear God's voice saying to us, *"Thou art my servant,"* we can answer with David, *"I am thy servant;…thou hast loosed my bonds"* (Ps. 116:16). But the Lord calls us not only His servants, but also His chosen ones: *"I have chosen thee."* We have not chosen Him first, but He has chosen us. If we are God's servants, we were not always so; the change must be ascribed to sovereign grace. The eye of sovereignty singled us out, and the voice of unchanging grace declared, *"I have loved thee with an everlasting love"* (Jer. 31:3). Long before time began or space was created, God had written on His heart the names of His elect people. He had predestined them to be conformed to the image of His Son and ordained them heirs of all the fullness of His love, His grace, and His glory. What comfort is here! Has the Lord loved us so long, and will He yet cast us away? He knew how stiff-necked we would be. He understood that our hearts were evil, yet He made the choice. Oh, our Savior is no fickle Lover! He does not feel enchanted for a while with some gleams of beauty from His church's eye, and then afterward cast her off because of her unfaithfulness. No, He married her in old eternity; and it is written of Jehovah, *"He hateth putting away"* (Mal. 2:16). The eternal choice is a bond on our gratitude and on His faithfulness, which neither can disown.

```
U O A D K S S P J P G F W I C B C P R O
L B R Y G A M E G D X C F A M I L Y C J
S E R V A N T R R Y R T L A M Y E I N W
K D H V O A U W A V O E A S I T Z L M Z
E I L V P U G N D A E R K B L Y N D W D
J E W L E X Y Z P F R P J N L W T F T T
U N K A C G M C G R V E E X C E B N L H
A C R S U C D H X G O R U D B F B C Q I
W E E A N O N O Z M V F W Y U G A O R S
R T C W Q M J S D Y O E I S G F D M S W
I S E A I M U E A H U C V T G M G F L I
T A I K E A L N N H Q T K F A C E O O L
T U V J L N N R D W M L X G I B B R H L
E B E C F D W H Z C O Y Q J R B L T U D
N Y D M H S S K Y M A Z B X F V D E V B
K B H E V E R L A S T I N G S H Z M M O
L O O S E D A Y Y H F H V L C R L C M N
K E I S D P K R X K N Z F U X H Q D F D
Z R U S P R A C T I C A L U J G W F O S
T T M O H C P R E D E S T I N E D T U O
```

CHOSEN	SERVANT	RECEIVED	PRACTICAL
UNPROFITABLE	BADGE	TABLE	COMMANDS
FAMILY	OBEDIENCE	HIS WILL	SERVE
PERFECTLY	LOOSED	BONDS	EVERLASTING
WRITTEN	HEART	PREDESTINED	COMFORT

Morning

*I have seen servants upon horses, and princes walking
as servants upon the earth.*
—Ecclesiastes 10:7

Upstarts frequently usurp the highest places, while the truly great pine in obscurity. This is a riddle in providence whose solution will one day gladden the hearts of the upright; but it is so common a fact, that none of us should murmur if it should fall to our own lot. When our Lord was on earth, although He is the Prince of the kings of the earth, yet He walked the footpath of weariness and service as the Servant of servants: what wonder is it if His followers, who are princes of the blood, should also be looked down on as inferior and contemptible persons? The world is upside down; therefore, the first are last and the last first. See how the servile sons of Satan lord it in the earth! What a high horse they ride! How they lift up their horn on high! Haman is in the court, while Mordecai sits in the gate; David wanders on the mountains, while Saul reigns in state; Elijah is complaining in the cave, while Jezebel is boasting in the palace; yet who would wish to take the places of the proud rebels? And who, on the other hand, might not envy the despised saints? When the wheel turns, those who are lowest rise, and the highest sink. Patience, then, believer, eternity will right the wrongs of time. Let us not fall into the error of letting our passions and carnal appetites ride in triumph, while our nobler powers walk in the dust. Grace must reign as a prince, and make the members of the body instruments of righteousness. The Holy Spirit loves order, and He therefore sets our powers and faculties in due rank and place, giving the highest room to those spiritual faculties that link us with the great King. Let us not disturb the divine arrangement, but ask for grace that we may keep under our body and bring it into subjection. We were not new created to allow our passions to rule over us, but that we, as kings, may reign in Christ Jesus over the triple kingdom of spirit, soul, and body, to the glory of God the Father.

```
G O P Y N G P O C X U S J H D K H F D I
U H O R S E S A J L S U Z W A Y X P A D
P M T S U C S C T Z B F I L P M M M A V
V S K G P L R O B I Y P R Z R W A Z W D
I K P W S S P U M S E O H A O R A N J U
M I A G T M V R F Z Y N G F V I Q L E S
E N L Z A C Z T B I W I C W I D C G Z U
T G A Q R Q O L S S V R J E D D A L E R
R O C Q T D O T S J E W Q D E L V A B P
D F E L S R Z E V H K G O K N E E D E L
H E V C C W E A R I N E S S C P S D L Z
G A E L I J A H K T Z C G Z E U W E I L
Z R X H D Y P V X W R M R I X C U N L C
G T Q T X K V R P M F P G W V B W M U
P H S D W D U M I J Z Z N X J N U C L R
P O R A G V E Y J N Z D I L W J X T S G
J U B F A K B A L M C B T P B E Z R I O
M M O U N T A I N B G E W H E E L R G D
Z M O R D E C A I A I L B K N O Y W B W
P R A Z X H M D T F O O T P A T H D N D
```

HORSES   WHEEL   UPSTARTS   USURP

RIDDLE   PROVIDENCE   GLADDEN   PRINCE

KING OF EARTH   FOOTPATH   WEARINESS   HAMAN

MORDECAI   ELIJAH   JEZEBEL   CAVE

PALACE   COURT   MOUNTAIN   PATIENCE

Evening

Marvellous lovingkindness.
—Psalm 17:7

When we give our hearts along with our charitable gifts, we give well, but we must often admit to failing in this respect. Not so our Master and our Lord. His favors are always performed with the love of His heart. He does not send to us the cold meat and the broken pieces from the table of His luxury, but He dips our morsels into His own dish and seasons our provisions with the spices of His fragrant affections. When He puts the golden tokens of His grace into our palms, He accompanies the gift with such a warm pressure of our hand that the manner of His giving is as precious as the gift itself. He will come into our houses on His errands of kindness, but He will not act as some austere visitors do in a poor man's cottage; instead, He sits by our sides, not despising our poverty or blaming our weaknesses. Beloved, with what smiles does He speak! What golden sentences drop from His gracious lips! What embraces of affection He bestows on us! If He had but given us pennies, the way of His giving would have gilded them; but as it is, the costly gifts are set in a golden basket by His pleasant carriage. It is impossible to doubt the sincerity of His charity, for there is a bleeding heart stamped on the face of all His benefactions. He gives *"liberally, and upbraideth not"* (James 1:5). Not one hint that we are burdensome to Him; not one cold look for His poor pensioners; but He rejoices in His mercy and presses us to His bosom while He is pouring out His life for us. There is a fragrance in His spikenard that nothing but His heart could produce; there is a sweetness in His honeycomb that could not be in it unless the very essence of His soul's affection had been mingled with it. Oh, the rare communion that such singular sincerity produces! May we continually taste and know the blessedness of it!

```
I C C Q Q E S E A S O N S D E P H C P Q
P S A N A U B D E J L H R O O X I N E R
Q K I P B N X G L G O W E L B B B V V R X
Z W I R N R G T C R V M R R L S X R F B
X K T N T F X U C A I C R S U J A C O A
H P E L D K W E C C N M A K X G Z T R F
J F W P H N S J T I G A N C U H G C M F
S L A D S K E V C O K S D H R I Z O E E
M T O K E N S S W U I T S A Y G V T D C
O I G J J T R J S S N E B R G P M T C T
R W W J T E U T X Z D R J I K R A A K I
S B U Z S P Z F L E N E G T C O Y G B O
E P H G B F R S C W E N B Y O V Z E Z N
L T Z J S K P E F O S N A T J I O X B P
S U S B H M Y W S Q S Y S U V S G D U K
X N Y Q D D L B C S W H K O U I D C A Q
I J O Y L F A V O R U Y E X N O N N Q O
H Z S G K G Y Q H Y S R T C T N O W D H
G O L D E N Z H D Y T N E K O I Z U Q A
Q M A R V E L O U S L D K J G I F T S O
```

MARVELOUS	LOVINGKINDNESS	CHARITY	GIFTS
MASTER	FAVOR	PERFORMED	LUXURY
MORSELS	SEASONS	PROVISION	GOLDEN
TOKENS	PRESSURE	ERRANDS	KINDNESS
COTTAGE	GRACIOUS	AFFECTION	BASKET

139

Morning

I drew them with cords of a man, with bands of love.
—Hosea 11:4

Our heavenly Father often draws us with the cords of love; but oh, how hesitant we are to run toward Him! How slowly we respond to His gentle impulses! He wants us to exercise a simpler faith in Him, but we have not yet attained Abraham's level of trust in God. We do not leave our worldly cares with God, but, like Martha, we burden ourselves with much serving. Our meager faith brings leanness to our souls; we do not open our mouths wide, even though God has promised to fill them. (See Psalm 81:10.) Does He not this evening invite us to trust Him? Can we not hear Him say, "Come, My child, and trust Me. The veil is rent. Enter into My presence and boldly approach the throne of My grace. I am worthy of your full confidence; cast your cares on Me. Shake off the dust of your cares, and put on your beautiful garments of joy"? But though we are called with tones of love for the blessed exercise of this comforting grace, we do not respond. At other times, He draws us to closer communion with Himself. We have been sitting on the doorstep of God's house; He invites us to come into the banqueting hall and dine with Him, but we decline the honor. There are secret rooms not yet opened to us; Jesus invites us to enter them, but we hold back. Shame on our cold hearts! We are but poor lovers of our sweet Lord Jesus, not fit to be His servants, much less to be His brides. Yet He has exalted us to be bone of His bone and flesh of His flesh, married to Him by a glorious marriage covenant. Herein is love! But it is a love that accepts no denial. If we do not obey the gentle invitations of His love, He will send affliction to drive us into closer intimacy with Himself. He will do whatever it takes to draw us closer to Him. What foolish children we are to refuse those bands of love and so bring upon our backs that scourge of small cords, which Jesus knows how to use to our benefit!

```
J Q K J L Z O O R W A C C M G F B O Q J
S B R I D E S P R T R O O L X M A T M S
U U G I V Z R F F E S N M P F A N E A H
H C C W M M D F E S L F F Y K R Q P R X
I L O E F P O U K Y I I O L W T U H R J
A V N V Z V U T A Y G D R E E H E L I L
W T X K E P S L R O R E T B K A T L E E
S E R V I N G Z S K R N I O A F H N D F
H V S Y N S A W U E N C N S Y G A E X O
J A B Q V U V N F G C E G W U N L P S W
G I R S I B C K T V Y C V J U X L O A J
T B E I T E U O L B V W O O D U F M B P
A Z S E A B T R R M Q H O P Q J E Z R X
T T P I T T T C D D F V K R H C U K A W
T V O H I I P N M E S V Q W L Q O X H J
A C N P O N B I R H N T N K B D V R A U
I Q D T N E X E R C I S E R W U L S M R
N I S Z N Y I L D L G H Q G K D P Y R G
T R U S T A C O M M U N I O N Y H B X V
P B Y T L B A N D S U S I P F J Z L R F
```

CORDS	BANDS	RESPOND	IMPULSE
EXERCISE	ATTAIN	ABRAHAM	WORLDLY
MARTHA	BURDEN	SERVING	INVITATION
TRUST	CONFIDENCE	COMFORTING	COMMUNION
BANQUET HALL	BRIDES	MARRIED	COVENANT

141

Evening

If so be ye have tasted that the Lord is gracious.
—1 Peter 2:3

"I*f*"—then this is not a matter to be taken for granted concerning every one of the human race. "*If*"—then there is a possibility and a probability that some may not have tasted that the Lord is gracious. "*If*"—then this is not a general but a special mercy; and it is necessary to inquire whether we know the grace of God by inward experience. There is no spiritual favor that may not be a matter for heart-searching. But while this should be a matter of earnest and prayerful inquiry, no one ought to be content while there is any such thing as an "*if*" about his having "*tasted that the Lord is gracious.*" A jealous and holy distrust of self may give rise to the question even in the believer's heart, but the continuance of such a doubt would be an evil indeed. We must not rest without a desperate struggle to clasp the Savior in the arms of faith, and say, "*I know whom I have believed, and am persuaded that he is able to keep that which I have committed unto him*" (2 Tim. 1:12). Do not rest, believer, until you have a full assurance of your interest in Jesus. Let nothing satisfy you until, by the infallible witness of the Holy Spirit bearing witness with your spirit, you are certified that you are a child of God (Rom. 8:16). Oh, do not trifle here; let no "perhaps" or "peradventure" or "if" or "maybe" satisfy your soul. Build on eternal truths, and truly build on them. Get "*the sure mercies of David*" (Isa. 55:3), and surely get them. Let your anchor be cast into that which is within the veil, and see to it that your soul is linked to the anchor by a cable that will not break. Advance beyond these dreary *ifs*. Abide no more in the wilderness of doubts and fears. Cross the Jordan of distrust, and enter the Canaan of peace, where the Canaanite still lingers, but where the land does not cease to flow "*with milk and honey*" (Lev. 20:24).

```
H R U Q D S A I N F A L L I B L E E F C
C S E T M P M S V K A H A N V E Y A A M
S O L B K E E G S E P H L H B N G B V G
D H E S Y C R E D U K U X O G H U H O D
O O W R D I C N A P R M F L N U W E R Y
C J J H L A Y E N Z F A O Y P D I X Q U
J S N R M L T R F F G N N W M X L P K R
E P A S W Q N A M O U R C C J T D E B C
A R V T N M O L J G E A S W E X E R F O
L O X S I G F G P J V C B R G Q R I K N
O B P Q T S P L R E X E K O I Y N E K T
U A G H H G F D B A M S W G P O E N J E
S B I B C O S Y Q L C W S I E J S C T N
H I V B I J Y S L Z N I S S Z Q S E S T
M L N R M D B D Y V N C O D O P R G Z C
G I N W A R D J E M U F X U D Y W Q C L
U T S C B A T A S T E X G Q S G O G L A
N Y M K H E A R T S E A R C H I N G X S
T R W W D T J O K G S Z X X C W Z F S P
T C M N P O S S I B I L I T Y Z H E G D
```

TASTE	GRACIOUS	POSSIBILITY	PROBABILITY
HUMAN RACE	GENERAL	SPECIAL	MERCY
INWARD	EXPERIENCE	FAVOR	HEART-SEARCHING
CONTENT	JEALOUS	HOLY	CLASP
ASSURANCE	SATISFY	INFALLIBLE	WILDERNESS

Morning

There is corn in Egypt.
—Genesis 42:2

Famine pinched all the nations, and it seemed inevitable that Jacob and his family would suffer great need. But the God of providence, who never forgets the objects of electing love, had stored a granary for His people by giving the Egyptians warning of the scarcity and leading them to store up the grain during their years of plenty. Little did Jacob expect deliverance from Egypt, but the corn in store for him was there. Believer, though all things are apparently against you, rest assured that God has made a reservation on your behalf; in the list of your griefs there is a saving clause. Somehow He will deliver you, and somewhere He will provide for you. The place from which your rescue will arise may be a very unexpected one, but help will assuredly come during your time of critical need, and you will magnify the name of the Lord. If men do not feed you, ravens will; if the earth does not yield wheat, heaven will drop manna. Therefore, be of good courage, and rest quietly in the Lord. God can make the sun rise in the west if He pleases, and He can make your source of distress the channel of delight. The corn in Egypt was all in the hands of the beloved Joseph; he opened or closed the granaries at will. And so the riches of providence are all in the absolute power of our Lord Jesus, who will dispense them liberally to His people. Joseph was abundantly ready to provide for his own family; and Jesus is unceasing in His faithful care for His children. Our business is to go after the help that is provided for us: we must not sit still in despondency, but rouse ourselves. Prayer will soon bring us into the presence of our royal Brother. Once we are before His throne, we have only to ask and we will receive. His provisions are not exhausted; there is corn still. His heart is not hard; He will give the corn to us. Lord, forgive our unbelief, and this morning cause us to draw largely from Your fullness and receive "grace *for* grace" (John 1:16).

```
E J R R N C D Y Z S E C V R U Z F W C D
V Y B T Z O X U Z A P J G X E A E O H G
S C S H A R Y P M V R J A J F S I Y A R
T U U A B N E G R I O E J C O E C L N A
G X F O G I A Y Z N V K W X O P V U N N
N R F I V N R J Z G I J I L W B A J E A
Q E E Q H S S Y G C D I G D X P T Y L R
S S R S L T O L M L E M D U Y F M F W Y
Y E E C Y O F L O A N T D E M A J R Y I
W R D A S R P V Q U C W E H B M M A L V
L V Q T Q E L W Z S E M L J M I A C O B
C A P R I Q E G Z E L O I Z A N G G U R
N T L O A G N T S N K D G B E N E A G
F I J D O D T P Z D K J H W N T I E W C
P O Q R L I Y K C A D A T B A T F G U J
B N Y L L L P I N C H E D C G S Y Y R C
N B D E L I V E R A N C E Y K A G P V H
Q F L Z S W G J X R A V E N S O U T B D
W H K K F J J R H Y P Z H F B O O V V A
G R E A T N E E D W K S C A R C I T Y F
```

EGYPT FAMINE PINCHED JACOB

SUFFERED GREAT NEED PROVIDENCE GRANARY

SCARCITY YEARS OF PLENTY DELIVERANCE CORN IN STORE

RESERVATION SAVING CLAUSE RESCUE MAGNIFY

RAVENS MANNA CHANNEL DELIGHT

Evening

The Lord will perfect that which concerneth me.
—Psalm 138:8

Clearly the confidence that the psalmist expressed here was a divine confidence. He did not say, "I have grace enough to perfect that which concerns me. My faith is so steady that it will not stagger. My love is so warm that it will never grow cold. My resolution is so firm that nothing can move it." No, his dependence was on the Lord alone. If we indulge in any confidence that is not grounded on the Rock of ages, our confidence is worse than a dream. It will fall on us and cover us with its ruins, to our sorrow and confusion. All that nature spins, time will unravel, to the eternal confusion of all who are clothed therein. The psalmist was wise. He rested on nothing short of the Lord's work. It is the Lord who has begun the good work within us. It is He who has carried it on, and if He does not finish it, it will never be completed. If there is one stitch in the celestial garment of our righteousness that we are to insert ourselves, then we are lost; but this is our confidence: the Lord who began will perfect. He has done it all, must do it all, and will do it all. Our confidence must not be in what we have done or in what we have resolved to do, but entirely in what the Lord will do. Unbelief insinuates, "You will never be able to stand. Look at the evil of your heart; you can never conquer sin. Remember the sinful pleasures and temptations of the world that besiege you; you will certainly be allured by them and led astray." Ah, yes, we would indeed perish if left to our own strength. If we had to navigate our frail vessels alone over so rough a sea, we might as well give up the voyage in despair. But thanks be to God! He *"will perfect that which concerneth* [us]" and bring us to the *"desired haven"* (Ps. 107:30). We can never be too confident when we confide in Him alone and never carry too many concerns when we have this assurance of His.

```
B J V E S S E L S U N P W P B O H B C D
P K F Y D C E Q U L W Z O G R D Q V O G
R P E R F E C T V K O B L O X D P A N O
S J T R G A W T V J W V L R R Z S C Q O
G M W E R Y Q P P Y S S E I N B A O U D
D F B S A P W M F O N T S G P S L N E W
R A F O C E M V I P S E A H R F M F R O
I I J L E F J O L J E A J T O B I I H R
U T C V U I F S B H D D F E C N S D S K
G H V E D X Q O W S G Y B O K D T E N E
A T Z D F B I B Q Q H K O U O J N N V C
R A S S U R A N C E D C I S F B I C U F
M D E P E N D E N C E Q S N A P E E Y X
E J M P O T X F N V E T I E G A O E O Y
N E G F L V A A I U T P A S E C N D X J
T G B W R H O W V R I K A S S N X T U H
M O C D Q A C V Q C E L E S T I A L I K
H O H E N I I Q Q M N Y S I P G V S C B
R U O W V F F L V O Y A G E X N O O I K
I X L O J G E Z K V G O D A L O N E Z Q
```

PERFECT	CONFIDENCE	PSALMIST	DEPENDENCE
GOD ALONE	GRACE	FAITH	LOVE
STEADY	ROCK OF AGES	GOOD WORK	CELESTIAL
GARMENT	RIGHTEOUSNESS	VOYAGE	ASSURANCE
RESOLVED	CONQUER	FRAIL	VESSELS

Morning

Henceforth we should not serve sin.
—Romans 6:6

Christian, what do you have to do with sin? Has it not cost you enough already? Burned child, will you play with fire? When you have already been between the jaws of the lion, will you step into his den a second time? Have you not had enough of the old serpent? Did he not poison all your veins once, and will you play upon the hole of the asp and put your hand on the serpent's den a second time? Oh, do not be so foolish! Did sin ever bring you real pleasure? Did you find solid satisfaction in it? If so, go back to your old drudgery and wear the chain again, if it pleases you. But inasmuch as sin never gave you what it promised to bestow, but deluded you with lies, do not be snared a second time by the old fowler. Be free, and let the remembrance of your ancient bondage forbid you to enter the net again! It is contrary to the intentions of eternal love, which all have an eye to your purity and holiness; therefore, do not run counter to the purposes of your Lord. Another thought should restrain you from sin. Christians can never sin cheaply; they pay a heavy price for iniquity. Transgression destroys peace of mind, obscures fellowship with Jesus, hinders prayer, and brings darkness over the soul; therefore, do not be the slave of sin. There is yet a higher argument: each time you "*serve sin,*" you have crucified the Lord "*afresh, and put him to an open shame*" (Heb. 6:6). Can you bear that thought? Oh, if you have fallen into any special sin during, it may be that my Master has sent this warning to bring you back before you have backslidden very far. Turn to Jesus anew; He has not forgotten His love for you. His grace is still the same. With weeping and repentance, come to His footstool, and you will be once more received into His heart. You will be set upon a rock again, and He will direct your steps.

```
X B Q S F G C E T B V F C Z D Z R E W D
P O I S O N A V P O Z Y L T G T E H M I
E C G W Z E S P Z U S I Q R S A C L Q R
K B T B Z K I R X D R N U L T I E I N E
J T H F S D R D H D N P Q Y N O I O D C
U H O L I N E S S G H L O X L U V N R T
A E T E R N A L L O V E R S D T E S U O
L R G L I G O R O J Z Z Y O E N D D D N
G Y Y F I C L C Z H O O P P C S M E G I
C I W H B F G Y O P N X I J C K T N E W
R Z H N U J C K I S Z D T Y K M L V R S
N F W I R T A F S B T Q F U C E C B Y T
U A R F N O Q W Q Y B M F O V H Y D B O
C Y A Q E E Q T S H F S F Z O L A M G M
L O K M D P N R F A C Z O N A L X I Z W
P Y X P L E A S U R E Q D S C N I O N B
P T O G N K E P U R I T Y Z Y N O S Z S
K U N Y R U T N D B B Z H E A R T G H F
S A T I S F A C T I O N N Y Z J D P K K
U S E R P E N T F E X Y M C S T E P S Q
```

COST	BURNED	JAWS	LION'S DEN
SERPENT	POISON	FOOLISH	PLEASURE
SATISFACTION	DRUDGERY	CHAIN	ETERNAL LOVE
PURITY	HOLINESS	PURPOSES	RECEIVED
ROCK	DIRECT	STEPS	HEART

Evening

Who healeth all thy diseases.
—Psalm 103:3

Humbling as is the statement, yet the fact is certain that we are all more or less suffering under the disease of sin. What a comfort it is to know that we have a Great Physician who is both willing and able to heal us! Let us think about Him for a while tonight. His cures are very speedy; there is life in a look at Him. His cures are radical; He strikes at the center of the disease. Hence, His cures are sure and certain. He never fails, and the disease never returns. There is no relapse where Christ heals. There is no fear that His patients will be merely patched up for a season; He makes them new people. He gives them a new heart also and puts a right spirit within them. He is well skilled in all diseases. Physicians generally have some specialty. Although they may know a little about almost all our aches and pains, there is usually one area of medicine that they have studied above all others. But Jesus Christ is thoroughly acquainted with the whole of human nature. He is as much at home with one sinner as with another; never yet has He met with an out-of-the-way case that was difficult for Him. He has had extraordinary complications of strange diseases to deal with, but He has known exactly with one glance of His eye how to treat the patient. He is the only universal Doctor; and the medicine He gives is the only true remedy, healing in every instance. Whatever our spiritual malady may be, we should go at once to this Divine Physician. There is no brokenness of heart that Jesus cannot bind up. His blood *"cleanseth us from all sin"* (1 John 1:7). If we think of the countless number who have been delivered from all sorts of diseases through the power and virtue of His touch, we will joyfully put ourselves in His hands. We trust Him, and sin dies; we love Him, and grace lives; we wait for Him, and grace is strengthened; we see Him as He is, and grace is perfected forever.

```
B R I M B A O D O C T O R S K T U M S R
F E V N S V Y Y Q D W D R U A D Z P G A
L I I G A U Z S N E P I N F P H G A J D
V U U E U P S P T P I T C F J R K T M I
F C O N A D E D E P F O E R G I I E C
P G O R Y G F E C R O Y D R I J P E D A
Z O K I A N L D R F F Z O I Q U I N I L
G M W C W L Q Y Y E M M H N A A S T C X
C V P E O T T Z F C T L T G K E U N I H
U S E R R M N U S T Z J F D A N N S N M
R G P S U Q F Z G E A I T N I U I N E A
E K V A I U B O J D T L G C X P V H H W
S G M S U R E X R M Z R L N X B E A A Z
H U M B L I N G H T N W E L L J R C X T
W Y V C E R T A I N R B G A B Y S H L J
L D W D M D H R L E I G O P T M A D V J
J Q I C O R I G H T S P I R I T L Y K S
V I R T U E Y X N E W P E O P L E O L E
C E H Q R E L A P S E U I I Y H Z Y B P
J M S X S Z M A L A D Y J N W F X V X T
```

HUMBLING   SUFFERING   COMFORT   CURES

SPEEDY   RADICAL   SURE   CERTAIN

RELAPSE   NEW PEOPLE   RIGHT SPIRIT   MEDICINE

TREAT   PATIENT   UNIVERSAL   DOCTOR

MALADY   POWER   VIRTUE   PERFECTED

Morning

He will make her wilderness like Eden.
—Isaiah 51:3

I see a vision of a howling wilderness, a great and terrible desert like the Sahara. I see nothing in it to relieve the eye. Everywhere I look, I am wearied with a vision of hot, arid sand, strewn with ten thousand bleaching skeletons of wretched men who have died in anguish, having lost their way in the merciless wasteland. What an appalling sight! How horrible! It is a sea of sand without end and without an oasis, a cheerless graveyard for a forlorn race! But behold and wonder! Suddenly I see, springing up from the scorching sand, a plant of renown. As it grows, it buds. The bud expands. It is a rose, and at its side, a lily bows its modest head. Miracle of miracles! As the fragrance of these flowers is diffused, the wilderness is transformed into a fruitful field; all around, it blossoms exceedingly. The glory of Lebanon is given to it, the excellency of Carmel and Sharon. Do not call it the Sahara; call it Paradise. Do not speak of it any longer as the valley of death's shadow; for where the skeletons lay bleaching in the sun, behold a resurrection is proclaimed. The dead spring up and become a mighty army, full of eternal life. Jesus is that plant of renown, and His presence makes all things new. Each individual's salvation is no less than a miracle. Yonder I see you, dear reader, cast out, an unswaddled, unwashed infant, defiled with your own blood and left to be food for beasts of prey. But a jewel has been thrown into your heart by a divine hand, and for its sake, you have been pitied and tended by divine providence. You are washed and cleansed from your defilement. You are adopted into heaven's family. The fair seal of love is on your forehead, and the ring of faithfulness is on your hand. Now, you are a prince unto God, though once you were an orphan who had been cast away. Highly value the matchless power and grace that changes deserts into gardens and makes the barren heart sing for joy.

```
L N R Y F T J P Q H I C Z P A U R E B B
F P G E L O E A N F U P X L R W Q I R L
H I N B D D Y R G E F C F A I N W X E O
R D E S E E D A R R O F V N D B S P A S
O C B L B H N D B I E A P T S H M H C S
U N K Z D C G I N Y B A T O S S O D H O
I F A Y T Z W S Q J C L T F I K Y R I M
P W I B W C I E O Y W Y E R K A S M N S
B L G P P L F Q C U D U X E N N F G T
L Q F R U I T F U L T M T N B C J V X G
H D M E R C I L E S S H S O T L V A I C
R E S U R R E C T I O N P W A N D U L U
J T Q W I L D E R N E S S N D D Y D D G
F L E B A N O N S H A R O N V H H E H K
U X Z A D H I L G R C M I C L G G S N E
X V A C W E A R I E D R B C U L J E G Q
X Z K O H A G W A S T E L A N D H R L F
E C A R M E L S F Q Z H D M C S L T I L
G H O W L I N G I O V C G Z G Y A A M L
K Z E P M A E N G F Z W N S W N O Q L Y
```

WILDERNESS	EDEN	HOWLING	GREAT
TERRIBLE	DESERT	WEARIED	ARID
BREACHING	MERCILESS	WASTELAND	PLANT OF RENOWN
FRUITFUL	FIELD	BLOSSOMS	LEBANON
CARMEL	SHARON	PARADISE	RESURRECTION

Evening

For the flesh lusteth against the Spirit,
and the Spirit against the flesh.
—Galatians 5:17

In every believer's heart there is a constant struggle between the old nature and the new. The old nature is very active, and it loses no opportunity of plying all the weapons of its deadly armory against newborn grace; while, on the other hand, the new nature is ever on the watch to resist and destroy its enemy. Grace within us will employ prayer, faith, hope, and love to cast out the evil. It takes to it the *"whole armour of God"* (Eph. 6:11) and wrestles earnestly. These two opposing natures will never cease to struggle as long as we are in this world. Bunyan's pilgrim, Christian, battled with Apollyon for three hours, but Christian's battle with himself lasted all the way from the Wicket Gate to the river Jordan. The enemy is so securely entrenched within us that he can never be driven out while we are in this body. Although we are troubled, and often in sore conflict, we have an almighty Helper, even Jesus, the Captain of our salvation. He is ever with us and assures us that we will eventually be *"more than conquerors through him"* (Rom. 8:37). With such assistance the newborn nature is more than a match for its foes. Are you fighting with the adversary today? Are Satan, the world, and the flesh all against you? Do not be discouraged or dismayed. Fight on, for God Himself is with you! Jehovah-Nissi is your banner, and Jehovah-Rophi is the healer of your wounds. Fear not, for you will overcome. Who can defeat Omnipotence? Fight on, *"looking unto Jesus"* (Heb. 12:2). Though the conflict is long and stern, sweet will be the victory and glorious the promised reward.

From strength to strength go on;
    Wrestle, and fight, and pray,
Tread all the powers of darkness down,
    And win the well-fought day.

```
M  H  U  R  E  S  I  S  T  Z  Y  B  M  C  B  O  L  R  M  U
Y  N  E  U  T  K  K  X  G  M  X  O  K  A  A  C  I  E  O  I
V  J  J  L  M  I  M  K  Y  B  W  H  R  Y  F  A  A  V  H  U
D  E  U  B  P  S  B  T  H  L  A  E  F  H  H  P  R  J  A  N
U  H  S  U  H  E  R  N  A  C  X  U  Z  S  M  T  M  Y  D  G
V  O  P  N  Z  K  R  E  R  P  A  P  F  N  M  A  O  D  W  I
X  V  R  Y  Z  B  A  W  U  O  O  J  Q  V  W  I  R  V  O  T
T  A  E  A  I  E  Z  B  T  D  E  L  K  P  I  N  O  J  P  O
Z  H  J  N  H  X  R  O  P  P  Y  B  L  B  O  K  F  F  M  W
W  N  X  W  C  M  C  R  R  X  R  F  Q  Y  A  R  G  M  H  E
H  I  E  M  A  J  C  N  K  E  D  A  V  B  O  F  O  N  O  U
W  S  M  S  T  R  U  G  G  L  E  O  Y  T  M  N  D  X  P  O
R  S  P  Z  J  K  E  R  Y  R  V  Z  V  E  A  N  C  C  E  B
E  I  L  Y  O  A  G  A  Q  N  Y  A  K  H  R  F  F  I  C  W
S  Y  O  S  R  P  W  C  N  S  U  G  P  C  F  A  I  M  M  I
T  K  Y  D  D  F  O  E  A  B  X  L  Z  G  J  I  B  X  P  C
L  O  C  O  A  W  V  F  F  U  O  L  D  N  A  T  U  R  E  K
E  O  S  K  N  L  J  J  O  T  B  G  L  E  P  H  P  O  K  E
S  D  R  Z  D  E  S  T  R  O  Y  F  T  D  I  L  O  V  E  T
P  I  L  G  R  I  M  M  E  K  B  U  C  I  C  D  F  T  C  T
```

STRUGGLE	OLD NATURE	NEWBORN GRACE	RESIST
DESTROY	EMPLOY	PRAYER	FAITH
HOPE	LOVE	ARMOR OF GOD	WRESTLES
BUNYAN	PILGRIM	APOLLYON	WICKET
JORDAN	HELPER	CAPTAIN	JEHOVAH NISSI

Morning

Good Master.
—Matthew 19:16

If the young man in the Gospel used this title in speaking to our Lord, how much more aptly may I address Him this way! He is indeed my Master in both senses, a ruling Master and a teaching Master. I delight to run His errands and to sit at His feet. I am both His servant and His disciple, and I count it my highest honor to acknowledge both relationships. If He would ask me why I call Him *"good,"* I would have a ready answer. It is true that *"there is none good but one, that is, God"* (Matt. 19:17), but then He is God, and all the goodness of deity shines forth in Him. In my experience, I have found Him good, so good, indeed, that all the good I have has come to me through Him. He was good to me when I was dead in sin, for He raised me by His Spirit's power. He has been good to me in all my needs, trials, struggles, and sorrows. There could never be a better Master, for His service is freedom, and His rule is love. I wish I were one-thousandth part as good a servant. When He teaches me as my Rabbi, He is unspeakably good. His doctrine is divine, His manner is gracious, and His spirit is gentleness itself. No error mingles with His instruction; the golden truth that He brings forth is pure, and all His teachings lead to goodness, sanctifying as well as edifying the disciple. Angels find Him a good Master and delight to pay their homage at His footstool. The ancient saints proved Him to be a good Master, and each of them rejoiced to sing, "I am Your servant, Lord!" My own humble testimony must certainly be to the same effect. I will give this witness before my friends and neighbors, for possibly they may be led by my testimony to seek my Lord Jesus as their Master. Oh, that they would do so! They would never regret so wise a choice. If they would but take His easy yoke, they would find themselves in so royal a service that they would enlist in it forever.

```
G D L A L L G O O D E G M A M C K B W A
J S E Q T D V A O C R X O K S S P T U P
L V W L P M Y G V E R X F S P U H L S S
T E S T I M O N Y Y A O H J P C U B O T
U Q I Y Z G P H T I N L I S R E W S R R
N W H C P R H Q O W D H O M U P L N R U
R K R T K E N T B N S N H D L J P Z O G
T A I S T A Z P M Y O H M Z I O I J W G
O C B W U D Q T V O E R F Q N U I M S L
D Q S B A Y F A H U S R R W G G O H Z E
D Q F F I A K N T N L M H H B E B U R S
Z O W O I N G I W G T R I A L S M F T Y
Y L E W B S V L W M Z L T K P Z A A R W
R Z Z V U W N D I A R H A P L F R S E I
S C S W I E Z V Q N S S W N U J W T E F
E V R V V R E X P E R I E N C E D E D R
U O V A D F O O T S T O O L I V G R O U
R E L A T I O N S H I P V F A F T L M U
T T F N Y Z C Q K L P I S A R M P J G V
T T E A C H I N G N G O O D N E S S U U
```

MASTER	YOUNG MAN	GOSPEL	TESTIMONY
RULING	TEACHING	DELIGHT	ERRANDS
HONOR	RELATIONSHIP	READY ANSWER	GOODNESS
EXPERIENCED	ALL GOOD	TRIALS	STRUGGLES
SORROWS	FREEDOM	RABBI	FOOTSTOOL

Evening

Behold, I am vile.
—Job 40:4

Here is an encouraging word for you, poor lost sinner. You think you must not come to God because you are vile. Now, there is not a saint living on earth who has not been made to feel that he is vile. If Job, Isaiah, and Paul were all obliged to say they were vile, oh, poor sinner, will you be ashamed to join in the same confession? If divine grace does not eradicate all sin from the believer, how do you hope to do it yourself? And if God loves His people while they are yet vile, do you think your vileness will prevent His loving you? Believe on Jesus, you outcast of the world's society! Jesus calls you, and such as you are. "Not the righteous, not the righteous; sinners, Jesus came to call." Even now say, "You have died for sinners; I am a sinner, Lord Jesus. Sprinkle Your blood on me." If you will confess your sin, you will find pardon. If, now, with all your heart, you will say, "I am vile; wash me," you will be washed now. If the Holy Spirit will enable you from your heart to cry,

> Just as I am, without one plea
> But that Thy blood was shed for me,
> And that thou bidd'st me come to Thee,
> O Lamb of God, I come!

you will rise from reading this evening's portion with all your sins pardoned; and though you awoke this morning with every sin that man has ever committed on your head, you will rest tonight *"accepted in the beloved"* (Eph. 1:6). Though once degraded with the rags of sin, you will be adorned with a robe of righteousness and appear white as the angels are. For *"now,"* mark it, *"Now is the accepted time; behold, now is the day of salvation"* (2 Cor. 6:2). If you believe on Him who justifies the ungodly, you are saved. Oh, may the Holy Spirit give you saving faith in Him who receives the vilest.

```
K N J B R D D R W H S K N Y V B Z S V Y
C I V K W W Q I S A I A H W S U B A D C
L U L A M B O F G O D V F L A H G V D S
T D I V I N E G R A C E B U I U O I E F
E B M O Y M G R D I R H Y D N Q B N R P
N K H Q X S X N E K B Z P M T H T G A Q
C Q O P D D P X D C A J L M W C Z F D B
O G G U X W W R N M E M E I Q M W A I J
U K B K T M Z K I W V I A O B K H I C F
R W J V X C K S Q N M A V L W S T T A H
A D H R C R A C B A K C W E M P O H T O
G X B I X H K S R U U L T U S V A O E L
I N Z M T G W Q T V L S E T O G C U D Y
N I J D U E P M U X P A R R G A O G L S
G Y V B L B M M X X J L E C G O N B Z P
K G J D P D A Z E F V V T S R U F U T I
T R V I L E S T T J U S T I F I E S D R
M L D P A R D O N O L Z K Q V P S N H I
C O N F E S S I O N O D G J N S S Y G T
O P S R Z R I G H T E O U S X F N Q Z I
```

ENCOURAGING	SAINT	ISAIAH	PAUL	ASHAMED
CONFESSION	DIVINE GRACE	ERADICATE	OUTCAST	SOCIETY
RIGHTEOUS	SPRINKLE	CONFESS	PARDON	WASH ME
HOLY SPIRIT	PLEA	LAMB OF GOD	WHITE	ACCEPTED
JUSTIFIES	SAVING FAITH	RECEIVES	VILEST	SAVED

Morning

Are they Israelites? so am I.
—2 Corinthians 11:22

We have a personal claim here, and one that needs proof. The apostle knew that his claim was indisputable, but many persons have no right to the title who still claim to belong to Israel. If we confidently declare, "I, too, am an Israelite," let us say it only after having searched our hearts in the presence of God. But if we can give proof that we are following Jesus, if we can say from the heart, "I trust Him wholly, trust Him only, trust Him simply, trust Him now, and trust Him forever," then the position that the saints of God hold belongs to us; we possess all their privileges. We may be the very least in Israel, *"less than the least of all saints"* (Eph. 3:8); yet since the mercies of God belong to the saints as saints, and not as advanced saints or well-taught saints, we may put in our plea, and say, "Are they Israelites? I am, too; therefore, the promises are mine, grace is mine, and glory will be mine." The claim, rightfully made, is one that will yield untold comfort. When God's people are rejoicing that they are His, what happiness it brings if I can say, "So am I!" When they speak of being pardoned, justified, and *"accepted in the beloved"* (Eph. 1:6), how joyful to respond, "Through the grace of God, so am I." But this claim has not only its enjoyments and privileges, but also its conditions and duties. We must share with God's people in cloudy times as well as in sunshine. When we hear them spoken of with contempt and ridicule for being Christians, we must come boldly forward and say, "I am a Christian, too." When we see them working for Christ, giving their time, their talents, their whole hearts to Jesus, we must be able to say, "I will give of myself as well." Let us prove our gratitude by our devotion and live as those who, having claimed a privilege, are willing to take the responsibility connected with it.

```
S Y M Z M T I T L E H N P E N R P P Q U
R J O O U L X O C K P J R N W Y Y P S A
P S C P E R S O N A L Q I J T Y Y U A V
I S R A E L I T E S S U V O R S V G I V
K W E L L T A U G H T I I Y X Z S C N C
O P O S I T I O N N D J L M U S C H T O
I N D I S P U T A B L E E E N R S A S N
M M L L I K F O K M B V G N T Y A P G F
S C A Y A E I Z B E V J E T O G D P I I
R L L W S I E C Z R Q O S S L H V I T D
N K F A A A M Q B C U O F J D C A N E E
I J P T I W D D J I P U T K C S N E D N
T E M H C M B V Q E T A P U O R C S K C
Y N B I K C P A E S V C R Q M N E S H E
W Q D H O T O R Q F G T J D F J D I R J
F T R E D E C L A R E C O B O K N U H A
S A P O S T L E R L L K W Z R N H T A V
N Q S E A R C H E D P Q A H T U E K E M
C T L U M G P J U S T I F I E D Z D W V
Q F U O S O D Q O Q L Z O I J O H Z J U
```

ISRAELITES	PERSONAL	CLAIM	APOSTLE
INDISPUTABLE	TITLE	CONFIDENCE	DECLARE
SEARCHED	POSITION	PRIVILEGES	MERCIES
SAINTS	ENJOYMENTS	ADVANCED	WELL-TAUGHT
UNTOLD COMFORT	HAPPINESS	PARDONED	JUSTIFIED

Evening

Ye that love the LORD, *hate evil.*
—Psalm 97:10

You have good reason to *"hate evil."* Consider what harm it has already brought you! Oh, what a world of mischief sin has brought into your heart! Sin blinded you so that you could not see the beauty of the Savior; it made you deaf so that you could not hear the Redeemer's tender invitations. Sin turned your feet into the way of death and poured poison into the very fountain of your being. It tainted your heart, and made it *"deceitful above all things, and desperately wicked"* (Jer. 17:9). Oh, what a creature you were when evil had done its utmost with you, before divine grace intervened! You were an heir of wrath even as others; you ran with the *"multitude to do evil"* (Exod. 23:2). Such were all of us; but Paul reminded us, *"Ye are washed, but ye are sanctified, but ye are justified in the name of the Lord Jesus, and by the Spirit of our God"* (1 Cor. 6:11). We have good reason, indeed, for hating evil when we look back and trace its deadly workings. Evil did such mischief to us that our souls would have been lost had not omnipotent love interfered to redeem us. Even now it is an active enemy, ever watching to do us harm and to drag us to perdition. Therefore *"hate evil,"* O Christians, unless you desire trouble. If you would strew your path with thorns and plant nettles on the pillow of your deathbed, then neglect to *"hate evil"*; but if you would live a happy life and die a peaceful death, then walk in all the ways of holiness, hating evil, even unto the end. If you truly love your Savior and would honor Him, then *"hate evil."* We know of no cure for the love of evil in a Christian like abundant communion with the Lord Jesus. Dwell with Him, and it will be impossible for you to be at peace with sin.

Order my footsteps by Thy Word,
    And make my heart sincere;
Let sin have no dominion, Lord,
    But keep my conscience clear.

```
B H M F N D W L U Y V G X U A G S H K S
Y E Q N O G R V Z M A P H P B G Y Y R L
O R A A E U L Q R A I N E D U P P M L O
M E G U V N N D E A F I J H N N M U Y V
O Y C B T M C T Q I J J Q B I D T Z L A E
M S X H L Y U B A P W T T C A M U T V T
Z I U P Y I K E K I H O E G N J Z I T H
X N U R X J N J I D N A R N T R B T W E
S T M A B G C D H N T G D K D F X U R L
K E I X C H A T E E V I L P I E L D E O
D R S P V D L J A D F I R X U N R E D R
A V C F Y B C V N O M R T T Q P G J E D
K E H N V H I K Z T Y A F A D K O S E L
A N I K P F Y F X A G W P E T B V R M E
X E E R M B A M X H K F S R I S H E I
E D F K M T A B P W C W B D K W O L R U
A R E A S O N B S H R J D B Q P U N B Q
C K E T J O B K C R E A T U R E Z A L O
L M G P E A C E F U L D X A Q H X R V O
M T H S A V I O R P E R D I T I O N X I
```

LOVE THE LORD   HATE EVIL   REASON   MISCHIEF

BLINDED   BEAUTY   SAVIOR   DEAF

REDEEMER   TENDER   INVITATION   FOUNTAIN

RAINED   CREATURE   INTERVENED   MULTITUDE

WORKINGS   PERDITION   PEACEFUL   ABUNDANT

Morning

Thou art weighed in the balances, and art found wanting.
—Daniel 5:27

It is well frequently to weigh ourselves in the scale of God's Word. You will find it a holy exercise to read some psalm of David, and, as you meditate on each verse, to ask yourself, "Can I say this? Have I felt as David felt? Has my heart ever been broken on account of sin, as his was when he penned his penitential psalms? Has my soul been full of true confidence in the hour of difficulty, as his was when he sang of God's mercies in the cave of Adullam or in the holds of Engedi? Do I take the cup of salvation and call on the name of the Lord?" Then turn to the life of Christ, and as you read, ask yourselves how far you are conformed to His likeness. Endeavor to discover whether you have the meekness, the humility, the lovely spirit that He constantly taught and displayed. Take, then, the epistles, and see whether you can go with the apostle in what he said of his experience. Have you ever cried out as he did—*"O wretched man that I am! who shall deliver me from the body of this death"*? (Rom. 7:24). Have you ever felt his self-abasement? Have you seemed to yourself the chief of sinners, and less than the least of all saints? Have you known anything of his devotion? Could you join with him and say, *"For to me to live is Christ, and to die is gain"* (Phil. 1:21)? If we thus read God's Word as a test of our spiritual condition, we will have good reason to stop many times and say, "Lord, I feel I have never yet been here. Oh, bring me here! Give me true penitence, such as this of which I read. Give me real faith; give me warmer zeal; inflame me with more fervent love; grant me the grace of meekness; make me more like Jesus. Let me no longer be '*found wanting*' when weighed in the balances of the sanctuary, lest I be '*found wanting*' in the scales of judgment." *"Judge not, that ye be not judged"* (Matt. 7:1).

```
O C P Y N D N C O N F I D E N C E L A U
U A O M E D I A T E Q R C U I T K I B S
H C D N L Y D E U G T B W L A N P K W N
A B V U F A E E N U Y J A T B B S E M R
Y C G A L O Z G A G R B J J O H A N A N
H W C D O L R Z S B E P L C P O L E E A
D M E O M N A M W V V D Y P Y L M S M M
G X N I U M D E D D E I M K Y S S O E
Q N J K G N I N D D B C I S S E N U D O
B Z F N K H T H E M T W H K A X N E J F
J B P S N A E P E N N E D J D E D T W T
Y E U T N G Q D K H H J F E S R P L E H
D Z P E N I T E N T I A L W C C H X O E
V K A J I E S A V P Z J C T A I U E C L
D L L I F E O F C H R I S T L S N E D O
T Q B R O K E N Q Q F X N L E E A L E R
P W W A N T I N G R U H B Y B N Q S C D
C U P O F S A L V A T I O N W K L I T K
H J U M Q N N P T J G O D S W O R D P L
Y V X H B A L A N C E S W E J I D D S M
```

WEIGHED   BALANCES   WANTING   SCALE

GOD'S WORD   HOLY EXERCISE   MEDIATE   BROKEN

ACCOUNT   PENNED   PENITENTIAL   PSALMS

CONFIDENCE   ADULLAM   ENGEDI   CUP OF SALVATION

NAME OF THE LORD   LIFE OF CHRIST   CONFORMED   LIKENESS

Evening

Who hath saved us, and called us with an holy calling.
—2 Timothy 1:9

The apostle used the perfect tense when he wrote, "*Who hath saved us,*" which indicates that the action had already been completed. Believers in Christ Jesus are saved. They are not looked on as persons who are in a hopeful state in which they may ultimately be saved, but they are already saved. Salvation is not a blessing to be enjoyed on the deathbed and to be sung of in a future state above; it is a matter promised to be obtained, received, and enjoyed now. The Christian is perfectly saved in God's purpose. God has ordained him unto salvation, and that purpose is complete. He is saved also because of the price that has been paid for him. "*It is finished*" (John 19:30) was the cry of the Savior before He died. The believer is also perfectly saved in His covenant Head, for as he fell in Adam, so he lives in Christ. This complete salvation is accompanied by a holy calling. Those whom the Savior saved on the cross are in due time effectively called by the power of God the Holy Spirit to holiness. They leave their sins, and they endeavor to be like Christ. They choose holiness, not out of any compulsion, but from the influence of a new nature, which leads them to rejoice in holiness just as naturally as before they delighted in sin. God neither chose them nor called them because they were holy, but He called them so that they might be holy, and holiness is the beauty produced by His workmanship in them. The Christlike qualities that we see in a believer are as much the work of God as the Atonement itself. Thus the fullness of the grace of God is brought out very sweetly. Salvation must be of grace, because the Lord is the Author of it. What motive but grace could move Him to save the guilty? Salvation must be of grace, because the Lord works in such a way that our righteousness is forever excluded. The believer's privilege is a present salvation; the evidence that he is called to it is his holy life.

```
O H N X V B V B U U H D S L J J R W B E
L T O Y Y R C D W C B E Y E T D P P E S
F I F L A M B L E V X L N P E S P L L M
Y C M S Y T O N J X U I A J X W X J I W
V K O G E C O Q B L U G A P O A Y Q E O
G T P M W V A N R L B H R R G Y F Y V R
F O U R P H J L E O D T N E A B E G E K
M I D E I L C V L M H E S C C I Z D R M
W Y N S C C E O P I E D Y E T T T Q S A
K H N I P O E T V R N N M I I T E C J N
A P S E S U M P E E O G T V O V N Q W S
N L H W L H R P A Y N M K E N M D Z K H
U X L W V N E P L I N A I D O S E L B I
A D R T Y Y J D O E D O N S A K A I Z P
V D C W Z X A L T S T X V T E C V Y V F
E X R V B B M B W Z E E Y H H D O S M B
A L R E A D Y S A V E D D Z I E R U Y Q
V E O A D A M P M K F M E K X J A B Z U
Y H A S D R S Y L I B T U N T R T D Q B
T V C D Q O B T A I N E D B E A U T Y P
```

HOLY CALLING	ACTION	COMPLETED	BELIEVERS
ALREADY SAVED	PROMISED	OBTAINED	RECEIVED
ENJOYED	GOD'S PURPOSE	COMPLETE	PRICE PAID
FINISHED	COVENANT HEAD	ADAM	ATONEMENT
ENDEAVOR	DELIGHTED	WORKMANSHIP	BEAUTY

Morning

O Lord, to us belongeth confusion of face…because
we have sinned against thee.
—Daniel 9:8

A deep sense and clear sight of sin, its hideousness, and the punishment that it deserves should make us bow low before the throne. We have sinned as Christians. It should not be so! Favored as we have been, we have been ungrateful. Privileged beyond most, we have not brought forth fruit in proportion. Who is there, although he may long have been engaged in Christian warfare, that will not blush when he looks back upon the past? As for our days before we were saved, may they be forgiven and forgotten. Yet, since then, though we have not sinned as before, we have sinned against light and against love—light that has really penetrated our minds and love in which we have rejoiced. Oh, the atrocity of the sin of a pardoned soul! An unpardoned sinner sins cheaply compared with the sin of one of God's own elect, who has had communion with Christ and leaned his head on Jesus' bosom. Look at David. Many will talk about his sin, but I trust you will look at his repentance. Hear his broken bones as each one of them moans out its sorrowful confession! See his tears as they fall on the ground, and hear the deep sighs with which he accompanies the softened music of his harp! We have sinned. Let us, therefore, seek the spirit of repentance. Look again at Peter. We speak much of Peter's denying his Master. Remember, it is written, Peter *"wept bitterly"* (Matt. 26:75). Have we no denials of our Lord to be lamented with tears? These sins of ours, before and after conversion, would send us to the place of inextinguishable fire if it were not for the sovereign mercy that has made us different. It has snatched us like burning wood from the fire. My soul, bow down under a sense of your natural sinfulness, and worship your God. Admire the grace that saves you, the mercy that spares you, and the love that pardons you!

```
X G S X G W E P H G H O U Y U Q C I E Y
W R P M X S Z R G V F L M B K S W C P K
A E A G E P B O C Z Y V F R Q R C F R J
H P R Q L G E P V D I C D O C N L I I V
M E E D E Y N O Z L C R K U U O E R V K
C N D E C Z G R T W B F Y G N Q A V I O
E T X E T R A T N G D O B H G H R F L P
N A I P H W G I N I M R F T R A S A E Z
R N F S R T E O C K B G O F A R I V G I
W C K E E D N Q X J I V O T P G O E O
A E U N K T G D K O T V Y R E M H R D W
U E Z S A D A P V B B E O T F U T E X R
K V R E A A E Y Y I A N N H U S A D G U
C S C V D Q Y N Y S C P P G L I U Q E K
Z R P A A T C P Y G Q L F K G C N V N O
F C M F E P K Y E I L A M E N T E D X H
F O R G O T T E N T N Y L C T D S I C B
W W A R F A R E K W E G C I U X I V H X
P A R D O N E D L I A R F S E R T B K Y
T C O N F E S S I O N J D N O M N W U L
```

DEEP SENSE	CLEAR SIGHT	FAVORED	UNGRATEFUL
PRIVILEGED	BROUGHT FORTH	PROPORTION	ENGAGED
WARFARE	FORGIVEN	FORGOTTEN	PARDONED
ELECT	REPENTANCE	CONFESSION	HARP MUSIC
PETER	DENYING	LAMENTED	SPARED

Evening

And I give unto them eternal life; and they shall never perish.
—John 10:28

The Christian should never think or speak lightly of unbelief. For a child of God to mistrust His love, His truth, His faithfulness, must be greatly displeasing to Him. How can we ever grieve Him by doubting His upholding grace? Christian, it is contrary to every promise of God's precious Word that you should ever be forgotten or left to perish. If it could be so, how could He be true who has said, *"Can a woman forget her sucking child, that she should not have compassion on the son of her womb? yea, they may forget, yet will I not forget thee"* (Isa. 49:15). Of what value would be the promise—*"The mountains shall depart, and the hills be removed; but my kindness shall not depart from thee, neither shall the covenant of my peace be removed, saith the* Lord *that hath mercy on thee"* (Isa. 54:10)? Where would the truth be in Christ's words—*"I give unto ["my sheep,"* John 10:27] *eternal life; and they shall never perish, neither shall any man pluck them out of my hand. My Father, which gave them me, is greater than all; and no man is able to pluck them out of my Father's hand"* (John 10:28–29). Where would the doctrines of grace be? They would be all disproved if one child of God would perish. Where would the veracity of God, His honor, His power, His grace, His covenant, His oath be, if any of those for whom Christ has died, and who have put their trust in Him, would nevertheless be cast away? Banish those unbelieving fears that so dishonor God. Arise, shake yourself from the dust, and put on your beautiful garments. Remember that it is sinful to doubt His Word wherein He has promised you that you will never perish. Let the eternal life within you express itself in confident rejoicing.

> The Gospel bears my spirit up:
>   A faithful and unchanging God
> Lays the foundation for my hope,
>   In oaths, and promises, and blood.

```
G F T G B W B D C O M P A S S I O N U Z
F C M V N Q R P L U C K P K C C L M P H
L A C O N F I D E N T T G F O P P O H V
M E I Z U U B H W T U V Y A N J R U O W
L V T T U F Z Y U R T W H T V E O N L B
O C J R H A X M I U K H A H E T M T D A
V N B S Z F C R S T F F C E N E I A I N
E B Z Y H K U D Z H C Q G R A R S I N I
V G O G K I G L Q I X B G S N N E N G S
Y V Z D O N T G N T H T O H T A U S P H
C O R P G D P C R E P D H A O L L M Q Y
V B M V S N F W B E S P Z N F L B U X H
U O M T H E I X X X A S O D P I G Z V Q
H I L L S S J X U X B T S A E F A L Z M
C P O U Q S G B B A X F E Z A E W W Q H
E Q C A O W E I M Y D M N R C I A O H P
P R E C I O U S W O R D U Y E S S G F S
T X S E I R E J O I C I N G M J V H Z R
N E V E R P E R I S H Y G M Q G E L J M
T B D Z T U E V W E E X P R E S S G A N
```

ETERNAL LIFE	NEVER PERISH	LOVE	TRUTH
FAITHFULNESS	UPHOLDING	PROMISE	PRECIOUS WORD
COMPASSION	MOUNTAINS	HILLS	KINDNESS
COVENANT OF PEACE	GREATER	PLUCK	FATHER'S HAND
BANISH	EXPRESS	CONFIDENT	REJOICING

Morning

The LORD is my light and my salvation; whom shall I fear? the LORD is the strength of my life; of whom shall I be afraid?
—Psalm 27:1

"The LORD is my light and my salvation." Here is personal interest: "*my light*" and "*my salvation.*" The soul is assured of it and therefore declares it boldly. At the new birth, divine light is poured into the soul as the precursor of salvation; where there is not enough light to reveal our own darkness and to make us long for the Lord Jesus, there is no evidence of salvation. After conversion, our God is our joy, comfort, guide, teacher, and in every sense our light. He is light within, light around, light reflected from us, and light to be revealed to us. Notice that it is not said that the Lord merely gives light, but that He is light; nor that He gives salvation, but that He is salvation. He, then, who by faith lays hold upon God, has all covenant blessings in his possession. This truth established, the argument drawn from it is then put in the form of a question: "*Whom shall I fear?*" This question provides its own answer. The powers of darkness are not to be feared, for the Lord, our light, destroys them. The damnation of hell is not to be dreaded, for the Lord is our salvation. This is a very different challenge from that of boastful Goliath. It rests not on the conceited strength of the "*arm of flesh*" (2 Chron. 32:8), but on the real power of the omnipotent I AM. (See Exodus 3:14.) "*The Lord is the strength of my life.*" Here is a third glowing epithet; it shows that the writer's hope was fastened with a threefold cord that could not be broken. We may well accumulate terms of praise where the Lord lavishes deeds of grace. Our lives derive all their strength from God; if He deigns to make us strong, we cannot be weakened by all the schemes of the adversary. "*Of whom shall I be afraid?*" The bold question looks into the future as well as the present. "*If God be for us, who can be against us?*" (Rom. 8:31)—either now or in the time to come!

```
Y A Z D E O D E I K V H D G U I D E Y I
O J L N J J O Z B X C A S I J R O J S R
F R O N A O V G R K G O X Y Q E B Z E B
C Z S P D C Y E C O Z Q M Q H Y T S Q S
R C Z L A Y H O L D M Z R F L C U T O D
E U N A F R A I D M I N K A O T B R L E
F A O I A R K B R V Z D I W T R U E B C
L T V J W R B Y L Q V R P P P V H T N T L
E E U E N T O O K F C S B Z O G F G L A
C A C R V E T U S F A O R D X T Z T K R
T C A O X M Y F N E D Z A V R R E H H E
E H Q S C K E P W D K Z P L H N O N G E
D E A W C G K K I N G R W I T H I N T R
B R H O U F N P U T L N B G G C R N R K
S A L V A T I O N A C I H C Y Y K L P
J A L N D E Y D Z I A L F T D F M T U X
Q V O O R Z F F E A R H D E P W H O M E
Z K A S S U R E D V Y H I G A Y N Z Z B
X D P Y B Q M V X P C C I J G Y S P Z Y
Z B O L D L Y Y B C H A L L E N G E F V
```

LIGHT	SALVATION	STRENGTH	LIFE
WHOM	FEAR	UNAFRAID	ASSURED
DECLARE	BOLDLY	JOY	COMFORT
GUIDE	TEACHER	WITHIN	AROUND
REFLECTED	LAY HOLD	CHALLENGE	OMNIPOTENT

Evening

I am come into my garden, my sister, my spouse.
—Song of Solomon 5:1

The heart of the believer is Christ's garden. He bought it with His precious blood, and He enters it and claims it as His own. A garden implies separation. It is not public property; it is not a wilderness. It is walled around or hedged in. Would that we could see the wall of separation between the church and the world made broader and stronger. It makes one sad to hear Christians saying, "Well, there is no harm in this; there is no harm in that," thus getting as near to the world as possible. Grace is at a low ebb in the soul that can even raise the question of how far it may go in worldly conformity. A garden is a place of beauty. It far surpasses the wild, uncultivated lands. The genuine Christian must seek to be more excellent in his life than the best moralist, because Christ's garden should produce the best flowers in all the world. Even the best is poor compared with what Christ deserves; let us not put Him off with withering, dwarfed plants. The rarest, richest, choicest lilies and roses should bloom in the place that Jesus calls His own. The garden is a place of growth. The saints are not to remain undeveloped, always mere buds and blossoms. We should *grow in grace, and in the knowledge of our Lord and Saviour Jesus Christ* (2 Pet. 3:18). Growth should be rapid where Jesus is the Gardener and where the Holy Spirit is the dew from above. A garden is a place of retirement. The Lord Jesus Christ would have us reserve our souls as a place in which He can manifest Himself in ways that He does not reveal Himself to the world. Oh, that Christians were more reserved, that they would keep their hearts more closely guarded for Christ! We often worry and trouble ourselves, like Martha, with much serving, so that we do not have the room for Christ that Mary had, and we do not sit at His feet as we should. May the Lord grant the sweet showers of His grace to water His garden this day.

```
K F G K A R S D I S T D P M W R W O O J
Z N T U Y K E I F S S S L G I P A Y X D
L S R U B X E K Y G E E A R L R L U B S
B S E P A R A T I O N W C O D E H B N T
S L O Z N G K G K I W W E W E C W K R R
X R O C G T W F X W G C O T R I I Y U O
A E Z S H E O E I L A N F H N O T B L N
O T B R S Y N I S K R O B Z E U H G D G
W I R I O O B U F G D I E M S S E I L E
N R O R Y D M J I W E P A G S B R Z L R
A E A N V E C S X N N S U P W L I L K G
P M D V X Z W A L L E D T M G O N C F V
D E E Y J Q V K M N I M Y A V O G W A O
W N R Q G V Q P S L Z W L N U D L H A B
A T R K G S F W L A P C T I X D P E P L
R O B I E P S G F A P L C F N J A D V H
F E X C E L L E N T N M H E F H S G I N
E O C S F Q Q B D O P T M S V S H E P H
D R M X I Q E C L R V E S T O S N D A X
U N C U L T I V A T E D L O W E B B G N
```

GARDEN	PRECIOUS BLOOD	SEPARATION	WILDERNESS
WALLED	HEDGED	BROADER	STRONGER
LOW EBB	PLACE OF BEAUTY	UNCULTIVATED	GENUINE
EXCELLENT	WITHERING	DWARFED	PLANTS
GROWTH	RETIREMENT	MANIFEST	BLOSSOMS

Morning

Thou art fairer than the children of men.
—Psalm 45:2

The entire person of Jesus is but as one gem, and His life is all along but one impression of the seal. He is altogether complete; not only in His several parts, but as a gracious, all-glorious whole. His character is not a mass of fair colors mixed confusedly, nor a heap of precious stones laid carelessly one upon another. He is a picture of beauty and a breastplate of glory. In Him, all the things of good repute are in their proper places and assist in adorning each other. Not one feature in His glorious person attracts attention at the expense of others, but He is perfectly and altogether lovely. Oh, Jesus! Your power, Your grace, Your justice, Your tenderness, Your truth, Your majesty, and Your immutability make up such a man, or rather such a God-man, as neither heaven nor earth has seen elsewhere. Your infancy, Your eternity, Your sufferings, Your triumphs, Your death, and Your immortality are all woven in one gorgeous tapestry, without seam or rent. You are music without discord. You are many, and yet not divided. You are all things, and yet not diverse. As all the colors blend into one resplendent rainbow, so all the glories of heaven and earth meet in You and unite so wondrously that there is none like You in all things; if all the virtues of the most excellent were bound in one bundle, they could not rival You, mirror of all perfection. You have been anointed with the holy oil of myrrh and cassia, which Your God has reserved for You alone. As for Your fragrance, it is as the holy perfume, the like of which none other can ever mingle, even with the art of the apothecary; each spice is fragrant, but the compound is divine.

Oh, sacred symmetry! Oh, rare connection
    Of many perfects, to make one perfection!
Oh, heavenly music, where all parts do meet
    In one sweet strain, to make one perfect sweet!

```
I L V Y S T O N E S X D V O W X P R C M
Y M Y G W H R B D H B P I Z W H R O H P
W C M A Y K O S E A L M M N B X E A I A
R K B U T Q Y T X Z R N P E C M C L L D
E J F R T I B T Y U R Z R V D P I L D O
L M B H X A S H Q L M E E I X N O G R R
U C M T Q P B D E N R O S A U U U L E N
L O N E G E M I H A O Q S E L H S O N I
M I S V G P R R L N P C I X I A L R M N
Q P Z E U W E Q X I D T O V K D J I C G
D E R Q V B M R R F T S N N C Z V O S G
E L Q C S E S N S J O Y P Z Q L C U N U
T D E W I H R H I O U S V I M Q Z S T I
N G P G Q Q B A O A N D R A N R Z Z V J
P I C T U R E Q L T E N D E R N E S S N
X E U F A I R E R P F A U X D J A J N I
Q C U J O Z K Y E N I Y G L O R Y Q L O
L X U F A Z A T V L N G R A C I O U S A
A F B R E A S T P L A T E Y U M S W V H
L C O M P L E T E E T E R N I T Y B D N
```

FAIRER	CHILDREN	PERSON	ONE GEM
IMPRESSION	SEAL	COMPLETE	SEVERAL
GRACIOUS	ALL-GLORIOUS	HEAP	PRECIOUS
STONES	PICTURE	BREASTPLATE	GLORY
ADORNING	TENDERNESS	IMMUTABILITY	ETERNITY

Evening

Nevertheless the foundation of God standeth sure.
—2 Timothy 2:19

The foundation on which our faith rests is this: "*God was in Christ, reconciling the world unto himself, not imputing their trespasses unto them*" (2 Cor. 5:19). The great fact on which genuine faith relies is that "*the Word was made flesh, and dwelt among us*" (John 1:14), and that "*Christ also hath once suffered for sins, the just for the unjust, that he might bring us to God*" (1 Pet. 3:18); "*Who his own self bare our sins in his own body on the tree*" (1 Pet. 2:24), for "*the chastisement of our peace was upon him; and with his stripes we are healed*" (Isa. 53:5). In one word, the great pillar of the Christian's hope is substitution. His hope is in the vicarious sacrifice of Christ for the guilty, Christ being made "*sin for us…that we might be made the righteousness of God in him*" (2 Cor. 5:21), Christ offering up a true and proper expiatory and substitutionary sacrifice in the room, place, and stead of as many as the Father gave to Him, who are known to God by name and who are recognized in their own hearts by their trusting in Jesus. This is the cardinal fact of the Gospel. If this foundation were removed, what could we do? But it stands as firm as the throne of God. We know it; we rest on it; we rejoice in it; and our delight is to hold it, to meditate on it, and to proclaim it, while we desire to be moved by gratitude for it in every part of our lives and conversation. In these days a direct attack has been made on the doctrine of the Atonement. Men cannot bear substitution. They gnash their teeth at the thought of the Lamb of God bearing the sin of man. But we, who know by experience the preciousness of this truth, will proclaim it confidently and unceasingly in defiance of them. We will neither dilute it nor change it, nor fritter it away in any shape or fashion. It will still be Christ, a sure Substitute, who bears human guilt and suffering in the stead of men. We cannot or dare not give it up, for it is our life. Despite every controversy, we feel that "*nevertheless the foundation of God standeth sure.*"

```
S P X G E N U I N E F A I T H S T T R A
R N Q A H T O K M M W E Z D X T U D R V
F E S H H R K T P Y E L I O H A E A E I
X V G A P E V P L O V G D G N T S C C
K E A B H P Y Z A G A O S W Q D C Y O A
E R T H H B V C E C T C R E P S A Z N R
X T C M S C K L G G H G E L N U R E C I
P H F O U N D A T I O N V L B R D D I O
I E G A X X Z J O W H J K E F E I W L U
A L Q C P C N D M R N P Q D M Q N J I S
T E C R Z G G I V E N R K S T E A D N N
O S Q S J J L V H W B Q E Z C R L R G S
R S K M C H A S T I S E M E N T T O T D
Y S H Q S C K U M A D E F L E S H O F W
G S U F F E R E D X M V G W U F J M G U
V C P R K C G R E A T P I L L A R X K P
M S M F G A L Y A M O N G U S Z E H C V
P X N D U J T H Y X P F P M T L R W D S
S U B S T I T U T I O N P V Z W H M T M
P K B Q V I N C H R I S T A T R D Y E K
```

NEVERTHELESS	FOUNDATION	STAND SURE	IN CHRIST
RECONCILING	GENUINE FAITH	MADE FLESH	DWELLED
AMONG US	SUFFERED	CHASTISEMENT	GREAT PILLAR
SUBSTITUTION	VICARIOUS	EXPIATORY	ROOM
PLACE	STEAD	GIVEN	CARDINAL

Morning

He shall build the temple of the LORD; and he shall bear the glory.
—Zechariah 6:13

Christ Himself is the builder of His spiritual temple, and He has built it on the mountains of His unchangeable affection, His omnipotent grace, and His infallible truthfulness. But as it was in Solomon's temple, so in this; the materials need to be made ready. There are the cedars of Lebanon, but they are not framed for the building. They are not cut down, shaped, and made into those cedar planks, whose odorous beauty will *"make glad"* (Ps. 46:4) the courts of the Lord's house in paradise. There are also the rough stones still in the quarry; they must be hewn from that place and squared. All this is Christ's own work. Each individual believer is being prepared, polished, and made ready for his place in the temple; but Christ's own hand performs the preparatory work. Afflictions cannot sanctify, excepting as they are used by Him to this end. Our prayers and efforts cannot make us ready for heaven, apart from the hand of Jesus, who fashions our hearts aright. As in the building of Solomon's temple, *"there was neither hammer nor ax nor any tool of iron heard in the house"* (1 Kings 6:7), because all was brought perfectly ready for the exact spot it was to occupy. So it is with the temple that Jesus builds; the making ready is all done on earth. When we reach heaven, there will be no sanctifying us there, no squaring us with affliction, no planing us with suffering. No, we must be made ready here. Christ will do all that beforehand. And when He has done it, we will be ferried by a loving hand across the stream of death and brought to the heavenly Jerusalem, to abide as eternal pillars in the temple of our Lord.

> Beneath His eye and care,
>   The edifice shall rise,
> Majestic, strong, and fair,
>   And shine above the skies.

```
E E N A Z H F Q B Z T T M S R M P Z M X
I R E A D Y G R A C E R O O O A R S P N
S N T V P D E C V P P V X L U T E P A I
K F F F F L U O X L S T G O G E P K F R
M M V A T K E C M P F E X M H R A H F N
X K W C L B G B Z P M M N O S I R G E Z
B E B E A L E W A P X P T N T A E R C D
Q F O D D K I S X N M L M H O L D E T U
U S Z A Q N U B U V O E N K N S V H I F
O V S R Y G N N L M X N R Z E V H F O C
G R M S M Z K W O E X A C T S X Y S N S
I L R F U Q W X O O M N I P O T E N T R
J N R M S A N C T I F Y Q N Y G K D R A
C W F A W I R C C A O K M U H A U O J S
T R U T H F U L N E S S C O U R T S E N
U L F U V U N C H A N G E A B L E O A U
X Q N X L O B B U P A R A D I S E G P R
U K T Z Y Y R Z E C H A R I A H D G O Z
M K L Z X M O U N T A I N S R T F U U Q
B U I L D E R W I M U K K C K E A I A C
```

TEMPLE	ZECHARIAH	BUILDER	MOUNTAINS
UNCHANGEABLE	AFFECTION	OMNIPOTENT	GRACE
INFALLIBLE	TRUTHFULNESS	SOLOMON	MATERIALS
CEDARS	LEBANON	COURTS	PARADISE
ROUGH STONES	PREPARED	SANCTIFY	READY

Evening

That those things which cannot be shaken may remain.
—Hebrews 12:27

Many things in our possession at the present moment can be shaken, and it ill becomes a Christian to set much store by them, for there is nothing stable under these rolling skies; change is written on all things. Yet we have certain *"things which cannot be shaken,"* and I invite you this evening to think about them. If the things that can be shaken would all be taken away, you may derive real comfort from the things that cannot be shaken, which will remain. Whatever your losses have been, or may be, you enjoy present salvation. You are standing at the foot of His cross, trusting alone in the merit of Jesus' precious blood. No rise or fall of the markets can interfere with your salvation in Him. No breaking of banks, no failures, no bankruptcies can touch that. You are a child of God this evening. God is your Father. No change of circumstances can ever rob you of that. Although by losses, you are brought to poverty and stripped bare, you can say, "He is my Father still. In my Father's house are many mansions; therefore, I will not be troubled." You have another permanent blessing, namely, the love of Jesus Christ. He who is God and Man loves you with all the strength of His affectionate nature—nothing can affect that. The fig tree may not blossom, and the flocks may *"be cut off from the fold"* (Hab. 3:17). These things do not matter to the one who can sing, *"My beloved is mine, and I am his"* (Song 2:16). We cannot lose our best portion and richest heritage. Whatever troubles come, let us act like adults. Let us show that we are not such little children as to be cast down by what may happen in this poor, fleeting state of time. Our country is Immanuel's land, and our hope is above the sky; therefore, calm as the summer's ocean, we will see the wreck of everything earthborn, yet rejoice in the God of our salvation.

```
C E R T A I N Y A H H K T S C E X F I M
X W E T N L C F F X P Q T E H K E O Y L
A V Q P V P C P F H G X W T I I G O E M
M Y C T C Z G N E V P K N S L V O T Q W
L Y D U Q D G C C X O T N T D Q D O R R
J R I A N A G Y T R R O K O O F A F I O
C G E G V U J O I F T I U R F I N T P L
J I W A P Q E V O X I M S E G Q D H R L
E S R T L R S T N H O G M K O V M E E I
S I J C A C E Z A D N F T H D S A C C N
T N S J U H O S T X F L Y R U C N R I G
A N R H J M C M E K Z O Q Z E O X O O S
B K S R A K S D F N H C B X R E U S U K
L F U U U K G T B O T K H P S Y D S S I
E R S O B W E D A U R S G N R E Z W B E
B M B W W Z G N W N L T R E M A I N L S
A V D U O Q I F N F C N U R Q H G B O E
P O S S E S S I O N Z E K G J G D A O Q
J Z S M A N S I O N S O S E O N U W D H
Z O P Q J A O T T R U S T I N G U N V Z
```

SHAKEN	REMAIN	POSSESSION	PRESENT
SET STORE	STABLE	ROLLING SKIES	CERTAIN
REAL COMFORT	FOOT OF THE CROSS	TRUSTING	PRECIOUS BLOOD
CHILD OF GOD	CIRCUMSTANCES	MANSIONS	GOD AND MAN
AFFECTIONATE	FIG TREE	FLOCKS	PORTION

Morning

Ephraim is a cake not turned.
—Hosea 7:8

A cake not turned is uncooked on one side; and so Ephraim was, in many respects, untouched by divine grace. Although there was some partial obedience, there was much rebellion left. My soul, I charge you, see whether this is your case. Are you thorough in the things of God? Has grace gone through the very center of your being so as to be felt in its divine operations in all your powers, actions, words, and thoughts? To be sanctified, spirit, soul, and body, should be your aim and prayer; and although sanctification may not be perfect in you anywhere in degree, yet it must be universal in its action; there must not be the appearance of holiness in one place and reigning sin in another; otherwise, you, too, will be a cake not turned. A cake not turned is soon burned on the side nearest the fire, and although no man can have too much religion, there are some who seem burned black with bigoted zeal for that part of truth that they have received, or are charred to a cinder with a boastful Pharisaic ostentation of those religious performances that suit their character. The assumed appearance of superior sanctity frequently accompanies a total absence of all vital godliness. The saint in public is a devil in private. He deals in flour by day and in soot by night. The cake that is burned on one side is dough on the other. If it is so with me, O Lord, turn me! Turn my unsanctified nature to the fire of Your love, and let it feel the sacred glow. Let my burned side cool a little, while I learn my own weakness and lack of heat when I am removed from Your heavenly flame. Let me not be found to be a double-minded person, but one entirely under the powerful influence of reigning grace; for well I know if I am left like a cake unturned, and am not on both sides the subject of Your grace, I must be consumed forever amid *"everlasting burnings"* (Isa. 33:14).

X D U G A D P B Z G K T D P B K O N Y W
X E O N I C I F O E Z H V V D L Y T S F
F E V P T Z T V S F K O R D B P U B P R
P U R K E O E I I Q D U E H J B Q O I J
G Q Z C X R U G O N E G B V S B F D R S
C H J U H I A C M N E H E V B I I Y I R
I J J J F C G T H Z S T L A Y W Z T T S
C A V U A Z D Y I E E S L Z Y O L U Y L
J C A K E G U M L O D W I O A I B O E I
O A X I S Y H A C D N Z O H P N N U J A
G T C P O W E R S D A S N H V E E N Q I
M R N H S O U L A M V R V Z E V H C S M
H I B D M A D Y K G X R V F K S O O U D
K B W X R O A O B E D I E N C E N O K C
W L C O J P R A Y E R O A G X A S K K E
A E G I R B B T H O R O U G H T U E E N
C J A M Q D E O A W Q W W E Z G H D L T
M V D X X V S X E X Z E U G V C T M B E
O H S D E P H R A I M J T Y V P P V Z R
S A N C T I F I C A T I O N F Y T E D H

EPHRAIM	CAKE	UNCOOKED	UNTOUCHED
OBEDIENCE	REBELLION	THOROUGH	CENTER
DIVINE	OPERATIONS	POWERS	ACTIONS
WORDS	THOUGHTS	SPIRIT	SOUL
BODY	AIM	PRAYER	SANCTIFICATION

Evening

Waiting for the adoption.
—Romans 8:23

Even in this world, saints are God's children, but people cannot recognize them to be so unless they observe certain moral characteristics in them. The adoption is not manifested, and the children are not yet openly declared. Among the Romans a man might adopt a child and keep the matter private for a long time, but there was a second adoption that took place in public. Then the child was brought before the constituted authorities, and his former garments were removed. The father who was adopting the child gave him clothing suitable to the child's new station in life. *"Beloved, now are we the sons of God, and it doth not yet appear what we shall be"* (1 John 3:2). We are not yet arrayed in the apparel that befits the royal family of heaven. We are wearing in this flesh and blood just what we wore as the sons of Adam. But we know that when the *"firstborn among many brethren"* (Rom. 8:29) appears, *"we shall be like him; for we shall see him as he is"* (1 John 3:2). Can you not imagine that a child taken from the lowest ranks of society and adopted by a Roman senator would say to himself, "I long for the day when I will be publicly adopted. Then I will remove these coarse, plebeian garments and be robed as becomes my senatorial rank"? Because he is happy in what he has received, for that very reason, he longs to get the fullness of what is promised to him. So it is with us today. We are waiting until we will put on our proper garments and will be manifested as the children of God. We are young nobles and have not yet worn our crowns. We are young brides, and the marriage day has not yet come. But because of the love our Spouse shows us, we are led to long and sigh for the bridal morning. Our very happiness makes us long for more; our joy, like a swollen spring, wants to well up like a geyser, leaping to the skies, and it heaves and groans within our spirits for lack of space and room by which to manifest itself to men.

```
G J U F L E S H A N D B L O O D I N C P
X N J D O O Z I W B M O R A L S C B I N
C Z E G W D Z V C Y A Z G W F O H X E D
C F H W P U B L I C P A X I V N A R G R
Z H J S S W I I L I P D R L D S R M A N
C I I S H T N J S T E O U L E O A K R F
B A L L R P A F G D A P Y B C F C G M L
J R I R D F W T L J R T X E L A T W E M
B Y E G H R B Z I B A I N Y A D E A N S
Q J K T K I E B H O O O T T R A R C T O
T P N P H Z E N D L N N B R E M I K S N
T D D B B R M H N Q G Y M V D S S F M S
X E W N R U E W O I B E N H R D T A B O
F E E I A A L N R Z Y X Z Q P H I F F F
X V V Z B K E Z C L O T H I N G C H J G
F I R S T B O R N Y U Z S E C L S P C O
Z M A N I F E S T E D P Q F N X Q H R D
I D R P R I V A T E H C K M A O H M E L
V W H G I T J A K N Z S R O M A N S R B
E D A H E Q S E M K S U I T A B L E D V
```

ADOPTION	CHILDREN	MORAL	CHARACTERISTICS
MANIFESTED	DECLARED	ROMANS	PRIVATE
PUBLIC	GARMENTS	CLOTHING	SUITABLE
NEW STATION	SONS OF GOD	APPEAR	WILL BE
FLESH AND BLOOD	SONS OF ADAM	FIRSTBORN	BRETHREN

Morning

*A certain woman of the company lifted up her voice, and said
unto him, Blessed is the womb that bare thee, and the paps which thou hast sucked.
But He said, Yea rather, blessed are they
that hear the word of God, and keep it.*
—Luke 11:27–28

It is fondly imagined by some that it must have involved very special privileges to have been the mother of our Lord, because they supposed that she had the benefit of looking into His very heart in a way in which we cannot hope to do. There may be an appearance of plausibility in the supposition, but not much. We do not know that Mary knew more than others. What she did know she did well to lay up in her heart, but she does not appear from anything we read in the Gospels to have been a better instructed believer than any other of Christ's disciples. All that she knew we also may discover. Do you wonder that we should say so? Here is a text to prove it: "*The secret of the LORD is with them that fear him; and he will show them his covenant*" (Ps. 25:14). Remember the Master's words, "*Henceforth I call you not servants; for the servant knoweth not what his lord doeth: but I have called you friends; for all things that I have heard of my Father I have made known unto you*" (John 15:15). So blessedly does this divine Revealer of secrets tell us His heart that He keeps back nothing that is profitable to us. His own assurance is, "*If it were not so, I would have told you*" (John 14:2). Does He not this day manifest Himself unto us as He does not unto the world? It is even so; therefore, we will not ignorantly cry out, "*Blessed is the womb that bare thee,*" but we will intelligently bless God that, having heard the Word and kept it, we have first of all as true a communion with the Savior as the Virgin had, and in the second place as true an acquaintance with the secrets of His heart as she can be supposed to have obtained. Happy soul to be thus privileged!

```
J N J J Z D Z J A Q H E X P A N D S R U
M O D E S T X C P O Z N M A Z E O H P U
L X N H W E I B J Q E X F G O G L A L N
E R Y R K H L C H E E R L E S S S R A Q
P C G L W A O W N D O I D X F A I O N V
O Z M I G H T Y A R M Y C E J P T N T O
K R L I W O N D E R W O O K I R T U O I
Q Y A I D D C A A B E L M F Y S I Q F C
C S L I L D C H G V T E P U D I A X R E
Q A O J R Y E F U L X O A S I S Z B E X
G T R C Q F O R L O R N N N V C O G N U
U L A M X Q I O A W F U Y Q I M I N O K
N W N S E F U Z D I U V D C N S F I W B
Q I T W A L H D T H H C L X E W D P N L
L I F T E D U P Q U P P T V H B V P D E
V J M W O R D O F G O D R A A Y U E W S
F C B E H O L D E Z E K V D N H H O S S
U M E J D Q T M Y V N H K A D P I I K E
F S E A O F S A N D Z V S I B Y Q G K D
C E R T A I N W O M A N B L M Z J V Y K
```

CERTAIN WOMAN	COMPANY	LIFTED UP	VOICE
BLESSED	WORD OF GOD	SEA OF SAND	OASIS
CHEERLESS	FORLORN	BEHOLD	WONDER
PLANT OF RENOWN	EXPANDS	LILY	MODEST
CARMEL	SHARON	MIGHTY ARMY	DIVINE HAND

Evening

Shadrach, Meshach, and Abednego, answered and said…,
Be it known unto thee, O king, that we will not serve thy gods.
—Daniel 3:16, 18

The story of the bold courage and marvelous deliverance of the three Hebrew children, or rather champions, well illustrates firmness and steadfastness in upholding the truth while facing the teeth of tyranny and the very jaws of death. It motivates believers to imitate their example. Let young Christians especially learn, both in matters of faith in religion and matters of uprightness in business, never to sacrifice their consciences. Lose all rather than to lose your integrity, and when all else is gone, still hold fast to a clear conscience as the rarest jewel that can adorn the human heart. Do not be guided by a will-o'-the-wisp kind of policy, but by the North Star of divine authority. Follow the right path at all costs. When you see no present advantage, *"walk by faith, not by sight"* (2 Cor. 5:7). Honor God by trusting Him even when it comes to matters of loss for the sake of principle. See whether He will be your debtor! See if He does not even in this life prove His Word that *"godliness with contentment is great gain"* (1 Tim. 6:6), and that those who seek *"first the kingdom of God, and his righteousness* [will have] *all these things…added unto* [them]" (Matt. 6:33). Should it happen that, in the providence of God, you suffer a loss by following your conscience, you will find that if the Lord does not pay you back in the silver of earthly prosperity, He will fulfill His promise in the gold of spiritual joy. Remember that a man's life does not consist *"in the abundance of the things which he possesseth"* (Luke 12:15). To wear a guileless spirit, to have a heart void of offense, and to have the favor and smile of God are greater riches than the mines of Ophir could yield or the business of Tyre could earn. *"Better is a dinner of herbs where love is, than a stalled ox and hatred therewith"* (Prov. 15:17). An ounce of heartsease is worth a ton of gold.

```
Q G E A K V L S Q S H A D R A C H D V T
F W K S S T E A D F A S T P K Q X E U Q
K O X N J Z M H X C E P L Q H V M L P R
U U E E T B D Q K Q O P A X H A E I H A
R R I Q A Y R X V W R U N N S U K V O S
K T H E B R E W J Q X H R H H U C E L I
V U A Y H X G X X O M T E A V I C R D N
K B X G U I L E L E S S X Q G C O A U T
E G V W L W Q A L V V C A A Z E N N U E
I M I T A T E U B Y G D M O Y F S C P G
E W E L Q B F J G E G C P D E H C E R R
E V P S B I A I Y P D U L Q L Z I O I I
O Q Z R H P O O R G A N E D Q F E F G T
A S U L L A N G I M G O E U D P N D H Y
B J L C B V C Y J Q N I H G B N C E T E
O F V E Y G O H M F F E H I O Q E P T I
G M A R V E L O U S Y B S K L N Z L R E
C H A M P I O N S F O H N S D R T H A S
B S P X X Q T Y R A N N Y B J C X E E K
X H V U Q W C J E W E L A W U W X I H C
```

SHADRACH   MESHACH   ABEDNEGO   BOLD

COURAGE   MARVELOUS   DELIVERANCE   HEBREW

CHAMPIONS   FIRMNESS   STEADFAST   UPHOLD

TYRANNY   IMITATE   EXAMPLE   UPRIGHT

CONSCIENCE   INTEGRITY   JEWEL   GUILELESS

Morning

Get thee up into the high mountain.
—Isaiah 40:9

Our knowledge of Christ is somewhat like climbing one of our Welsh mountains. When you are at the base you see but little: the mountain itself appears to be but one-half as high as it really is. Confined in a little valley, you discover scarcely anything but the rippling brooks as they descend into the stream at the foot of the mountain. Climb the first rising knoll, and the valley lengthens and widens beneath your feet. Go higher, and you see the country for four or five miles round, and you are delighted with the widening prospect. Climb higher still, and the scene enlarges, until at last, when you are on the summit, and look east, west, north, and south, you see almost all of England lying before you. Yonder is a forest in some distant county, perhaps two hundred miles away, and here the sea, and there a shining river and the smoking chimneys of a manufacturing town, or the masts of the ships in a busy port. All these things please and delight you, and you say, "I could not have imagined that so much could be seen at this elevation." Now, the Christian life is of the same order. When we first believe in Christ we see but little of Him. The higher we climb, the more we discover of His beauties. But who has ever gained the summit? Who has known all the heights and depths of the *"love of Christ, which passeth knowledge"* (Eph. 3:19)? Paul, when grown old, sitting gray-haired, shivering in a dungeon in Rome, could say with greater emphasis than we can, *"I know whom I have believed"* (2 Tim. 1:12), for each experience had been like the climbing of a hill, each trial had been like ascending another summit, and his death seemed like gaining the top of the mountain, from which he could see the whole of the faithfulness and the love of Him to whom he had committed his soul. Get up, dear friend, into the high mountain.

```
M T M C L I M B I N G X C S D I Z O B O
I W P Z G M R L B A T J H I E U U A R V
L K R S H I N I N G R I V E R D N J O K
T U O C O U N T Y U W P H W E L S H O N
E K S S T N G X X T A S Y P E S I H K O
X H P L E N G T H E N M B O Z M X P H L
F Y E I C W I S E I E Z P U N H L J I L
E Q C C C O I J U C J G K C U D U V G R
Y S T O R A N D R M X Y F V M B E P H E
F C D K T B Y F E Q M X J V O K Y R M V
R I P P L I N G I N Z I H Y E Q W H O A
V C Z I M Y H J K N S D T W G F E T U L
H H K K G M I R H H E T M D B O X I N L
V Z M P I E G I E Y O D I S S R J K T E
A G U E B E H U R Q B O T O I E O F A Y
S C E N E K E V B D N Z E G H S Q C I C
K V U A Z L R J M O H A A E R T L J N R
Q B P W X X X F T X W F M O A J F J J K
E L E V A T I O N U A Z Z L O M A S O A
W P I H P S T R E A M N G H G Z F X N E
```

HIGH MOUNTAIN	CLIMBING	CONFINED	WELSH
RIPPLING	BROOK	STREAM	KNOLL
VALLEY	LENGTHEN	WIDEN	HIGHER
PROSPECT	SCENE	SUMMIT	YONDER
FOREST	COUNTY	SHINING RIVER	ELEVATION

Evening

The dove found no rest for the sole of her foot.
—Genesis 8:9

Reader, can you find rest apart from the ark, Christ Jesus? Then be assured that your religion is vain. Are you satisfied with anything short of a conscious knowledge of your union and interest in Christ? Then woe to you. If you profess to be a Christian, yet find full satisfaction in worldly pleasures and pursuits, your profession is false. If your soul can stretch itself, find the bed long enough, and the coverlet wide enough to cover it in the chambers of sin, then you are a hypocrite. You are far from any right thoughts of Christ or perception of His preciousness. On the other hand, if you could indulge in sin without receiving any punishment, but you feel that sin in itself would be a punishment; and if you could have the whole world and live in it forever, but you feel that would be true misery, for your God is what your soul craves; then be of good courage: you are a child of God. With all your sins and imperfections, let this thought comfort you: if your soul finds no rest in sin, you are not as the sinner is! If you are still crying for and craving after something better, Christ has not forgotten you, for you have not quite forgotten Him. The believer cannot do without his Lord. Words are inadequate to express his thoughts of Him. We cannot live on the sands of the wilderness. We need the manna that drops from on high. Our skin bottles of creature confidence cannot yield us a drop of moisture, but we drink of the Rock that follows us, and that Rock is Christ. (See 1 Corinthians 10:4.) When you feed on Him, your soul can sing, "He has satisfied my *'mouth with good things; so that* [my] *youth is renewed like the eagle's'*" (Ps. 103:5). But if you do not have Him, your bursting wine vat and well-filled barn can give you no sort of satisfaction. Instead, lament over them in the words of wisdom, "*Vanity of vanities; all is vanity*" (Eccl. 1:2).

```
D A B C N F C O Y Z E S V S F C T W U R
D I N O V K O R U S T F S O T D V G W I
A H Y X T E L O A Y W Y U L S E L C F G
T Q S E U G Q A F V P Y X E B L J V E H
S I U N O R E S T G E S W O T L P P B T
G A D V A V N D Z O L S K F O K E R P T
C Z T I W Q R N J O C R B H N F R O I H
G H I I E M N T F D T U C E V W C F P O
F R A N S O R V W T U X W R O O E E R U
P X W M A F H S R H C T K F S R P S E G
L T Y J B D I T L I M W Z O K L T S C H
E H X B A E E E B N I R C O N D I I I T
A K Q F A J R Q D G T P O T X L O X O S
S O X W Q T D O U S D K V D O Y N K U H
U J R Q F F Z C F A D R E P N N D O S G
R C I S K P A P U S T H R Y L Y L N N P
E Y C G L I D O V E I E L I E Y L Z E I
W H O L E W O R L D D N E H H W U M S F
Q I N T E R E S T B I S T R E T C H S T
U K C H I L D O F G O D K L U N I O N N
```

DOVE	NO REST	SOLE OF HER FOOT	WORLDLY
UNION	INTEREST	PROFESS	PLEASURE
STRETCH	COVERLET	CHAMBER OF SIN	RIGHT THOUGHTS
PERCEPTION	PRECIOUSNESS	WHOLE WORLD	CRAVES
CHILD OF GOD	INADEQUATE	SATISFIED	GOOD THINGS

Morning

Having escaped the corruption that is in the world through lust.
—2 Peter 1:4

Banish forever all thoughts of indulging the flesh if you want to live in the power of your risen Lord. It is immoral for a man who is alive in Christ to dwell in the corruption of sin. *"Why seek ye the living among the dead?"* (Luke 24:5), asked the angel of the women who came to Jesus' tomb. Should the living dwell in a tomb? Should divine life be buried in the mausoleum of fleshly lust? How can we partake of the cup of the Lord and yet drink from the cup of Satan? Surely, believer, you are delivered from open lusts and sins. Have you also escaped from the more secret and deceptive traps of the satanic fowler? Have you come forth from the lust of pride? Have you escaped from slothfulness? Have you made a clean break from carnal security? Are you seeking day by day to live above worldliness, the pride of life, and the ensnaring vice of greed? Remember, it is for this that you have been enriched with the treasures of God. If you are indeed the chosen of God and beloved by Him, do not permit all the lavish treasure of grace to be wasted on you. Follow after holiness; it is the Christian's crown and glory. An unholy church is useless to the world and has no esteem among men. It is an abomination; it is hell's laughter and heaven's abhorrence. The worst evils that have ever come upon the world have been brought by an unholy church. O Christian, the vows of God are upon you. You are God's priest: act as such. You are God's king: reign over your lusts. You are God's chosen: do not associate with the devil. Heaven is your portion: live like a heavenly spirit, and you will prove that you have true faith in Jesus. There cannot be faith in the heart unless there is holiness in the life.

Lord, I desire to live as one
   Who bears a blood-bought name,
As one who fears but grieving Thee,
   And knows no other shame.

```
P H E A V E N L Y S P I R I T M S H C I
C S T B A Z W T C Z M A S Q O R A J I A
V C A M X G B L L S S S B H M I U H C A
B K S Z A C S L A J T T G K L S G N E N
K V G H H U L D O U M Q H G N E Z Q H G
L H K O Q P S E N O G Y P H R N K C O E
E I D L V Q O O A X D H H R D L P R M L
U S F I W J Z R L N N B T B H O C O I N
U X T N C M K Q T E B R O E B R S W C O
T S R E Q J R Y O I U R F U R D L N O S
G Q T S E G W R G T O M E H G B X A R H
B Q E S H M L G R L C N A A G H J N R A
W E S C A P E D H F Z N K L K R T D U M
O L E B M K C H O S E N W Y C N U G P E
M R R G R I E V I N G P E J F Z Z L T L
E A L I V E I N C H R I S T A Y K O I R
N K D U G P U Y V O N H T C W X L R O O
F H E Q L I V I N G K F F R X R J Y N W
V G O D S P R I E S T P Z A C O C M Y W
Q J Y Y D Q J W F U R K B T V M E T T J
```

ESCAPED	CORRUPTION	RISEN LORD	ALIVE IN CHRIST
ANGEL	WOMEN	LIVING	MAUSOLEUM
GRIEVING	CLEAN BREAK	CROWN AND GLORY	HOLINESS
ESTEEM	PORTION	CHOSEN	HEAVENLY SPIRIT
BLOOD-BOUGHT	NO SHAME	LAUGHTER	GOD'S PRIEST

Evening

Looking unto Jesus.
—Hebrews 12:2

It is always the Holy Spirit's work to turn our eyes away from self to Jesus; but Satan's work is just the opposite of this, for he is constantly trying to make us pay attention to ourselves instead of to Christ. He insinuates, "Your sins are too great for pardon; you have no faith. You do not repent enough. You will never be able to continue to the end. You do not have the joy of His children. You have such a weak hold of Jesus." All these are thoughts about self, and we will never find comfort or assurance by looking within. But the Holy Spirit turns our eyes entirely away from self. He tells us that we are nothing, but that "Christ is all in all." Remember, therefore, that it is not your hold of Christ that saves you; it is Christ. It is not your joy in Christ that saves you; it is Christ. It is not even your faith in Christ, though that is the instrument, but it is Christ's blood and His merits that save you; therefore, do not look as much to your hand, with which you are grasping Christ, as to Christ. Do not look to your hope, but to Jesus, the Source of your hope. Do not look to your faith, but to *"Jesus, the author and finisher of* [your] *faith"* (Heb. 12:2). We will never find happiness by looking at our prayers, our actions, or our feelings. It is what Jesus is, not what we are, that gives rest to the soul. If we would at once overcome Satan and have peace with God, it must be by *"looking unto Jesus."* Keep your eyes simply on Him. Let His death, His sufferings, His merits, His glories, and His intercession be fresh on your mind. When you wake in the morning, look to Him. When you lie down at night, look to Him. Oh, do not let your hopes or fears come between you and Jesus. Follow hard after Him, and He will never fail you.

My hope is built on nothing less
    Than Jesus' blood and righteousness:
I dare not trust the sweetest frame,
    But wholly lean on Jesus' name.

```
L F J O Y O F H I S C H I L D R E N L L
H N A C R Q G Y I Q U Z Q N R F P U O I
S X S I V G H B Z X N M T C V N G F O N
E D D X T L I J V Q T Y N G M Y A R K S
M X Z M Q H S O J T O B K R M A P H I T
B M J I T X M Y F K J D V A X Y D P N R
R O Q I U E E T K O E H U S H B G Y G U
D E X B T S R P J R S G E P I O A D Y M
N R P F W L I N C A U U V I P O L S R E
E S Q E G J T S U A S Z G N A L L D U N
C D Y R N S S T U I T X F G R G I P E T
L I V J U T T F O K F B N K D W N O X A
T H O U G H T S O F S E L F O M A G O N
C H R I S T S B L O O D A Q N G L M Y E
D V B A S S U R A N C E F E P J L I T W
A N L C H O L Y S P I R I T X I M H Y G
E N S N N K Q N X H X G B Y V H O P E C
F S O P Z O T N M G C O N T I N U E N O
A Z E C S N V X W S E U U S O U R C E Z
G C O M F O R T F K O V H H E T N M N Q
```

LOOKING	UNTO JESUS	HOLY SPIRIT	PARDON
REPENT	CONTINUE	JOY OF HIS CHILDREN	THOUGHTS OF SELF
COMFORT	ASSURANCE	ALL IN ALL	HOLD
JOY	FAITH	INSTRUMENT	CHRIST'S BLOOD
HIS MERITS	GRASPING	SOURCE	HOPE

But Aaron's rod swallowed up their rods.
—Exodus 7:12

This incident is an instructive example of the sure victory of the divine handiwork over all opposition. Whenever a divine principle is cast into the heart, though the devil may fashion a counterfeit and produce swarms of opponents, as surely as God is in the work, it will swallow up all its foes. If God's grace takes possession of a man, the world's magicians may throw down all their rods. Every rod may be as cunning and poisonous as a serpent, but Aaron's rod will swallow up their rods. The sweet attractions of the Cross will woo and win the man's heart, and he who once lived only for this deceitful earth will now have an eye for the upper spheres and a wing to mount into heavenly heights. When grace has won the day, the person who once was concerned only with earthly matters now seeks the world to come. The same fact is to be observed in the life of the believer. What a host of foes our faith has had to meet! Our old sins—the devil threw them down before us, and they turned to serpents. What a great number of sins there were! But the Cross of Jesus destroys them all. Faith in Christ makes short work of all our sins. Then the devil has launched forth another host of serpents in the form of worldly trials, temptations, and unbelief; but faith in Jesus is more than a match for them and overcomes them all. The same absorbing principle shines in the faithful service of God! When one has an enthusiastic love for Jesus, his difficulties are surmounted, his sacrifices become pleasures, and his sufferings are honors. But if religion is thus a consuming passion in the heart, it follows that there are many persons who profess religion but do not have it; for what they have will not bear this test. Examine yourself, dear reader, on this point. Aaron's rod proved its heaven-given power. Is your religion doing so? If Christ is anything, He must be everything. Do not rest until love and faith in Jesus are the master passions of your soul!

```
W  I  E  T  S  N  H  Z  L  Z  U  T  I  N  N  Y  L  H  V  B
C  F  K  M  S  E  P  O  A  D  Q  P  N  F  U  N  B  W  J  C
G  R  R  X  H  O  R  K  N  I  W  K  C  G  K  U  T  B  D  A
N  B  Y  F  V  B  G  P  H  O  I  W  I  B  J  N  Y  W  M  M
C  E  M  Z  H  D  Z  T  E  K  R  Y  D  F  Z  B  R  H  A  H
N  R  N  G  A  A  I  L  P  N  E  S  E  G  T  E  W  Z  G  E
U  S  X  T  G  V  N  A  E  D  T  W  N  R  E  L  O  N  I  A
P  W  Y  X  H  C  V  D  S  N  I  S  T  H  M  I  R  L  C  V
P  A  P  U  P  U  K  C  I  X  O  T  Z  V  P  E  L  E  I  E
E  L  C  S  F  L  S  B  M  W  Z  A  G  I  T  F  D  G  A  N
R  L  W  U  Q  I  E  I  I  W  O  G  R  C  A  L  T  V  N  L
S  O  T  R  B  A  E  A  A  Z  E  R  R  T  T  O  O  H  S  Y
P  W  R  M  I  M  I  V  S  S  M  J  K  O  I  P  C  I  A  H
H  E  I  O  L  C  Y  S  I  U  T  N  X  R  O  W  O  B  A  E
E  D  A  U  P  U  N  B  B  P  R  I  U  Y  N  J  M  B  R  I
R  V  L  N  H  L  C  W  M  I  Q  E  C  I  S  V  E  A  O  G
E  Z  S  T  I  E  H  D  R  B  F  E  S  T  F  I  B  T  N  H
S  V  L  E  M  G  O  V  E  R  C  O  M  E  S  U  Z  H  R  T
D  W  M  D  P  D  C  R  O  S  S  O  F  J  E  S  U  S  N  S
S  A  R  A  T  T  R  A  C  T  I  O  N  S  J  V  W  G  A  V
```

AARON	SWALLOWED	INCIDENT	VICTORY
HANDIWORK	MAGICIANS	ATTRACTIONS	UPPER SPHERES
HEAVENLY HEIGHTS	WORLD TO COME	SERPENTS	CROSS OF JESUS
TRIALS	TEMPTATIONS	UNBELIEF	OVERCOMES
ENTHUSIASTIC	SURMOUNTED	PLEASURES	HONORS

Evening

Howbeit in the business of the ambassadors of the princes of Babylon, who sent unto him to inquire of the wonder that was done in the land, God left him, to try him, that he might know
all that was in his heart.
—2 Chronicles 32:31

Hezekiah was growing so inwardly great and priding himself so much on the favor of God that self-righteousness crept in. Because of his carnal security, the grace of God was, in its more active operations, withdrawn for a time. This explains his difficulties with the Babylonians; for if the grace of God would leave the best Christian, there is enough of sin in his heart to make him the worst of transgressors. If left to yourselves, you who are warmest for Christ would cool down like Laodicea into sickening luke-warmness. (See Revelation 3:16.) You who are sound in the faith would be white with the leprosy of false doctrine. You who now walk before the Lord in excellency and integrity would reel to and fro and stagger with a drunkenness of evil passion. Like the moon, we borrow our light; bright as we are when grace shines on us, we are darkness itself when the Sun of Righteousness withdraws Himself. Therefore, let us cry to God never to leave us. Lord, do not take Your Holy Spirit from us! Do not withdraw Your indwelling grace! Have You not said, *"I the LORD do keep it; I will water it every moment: lest any hurt it, I will keep it night and day"* (Isa. 27:3)? Lord, keep us everywhere. Keep us when we are in the valley, so that we will not complain about Your humbling hand. Keep us when we are on the mountain, so that we will not become dizzy from being lifted up. Keep us in our youth, when our passions are strong; keep us in our old age, when becoming conceited by our wisdom, we might prove greater fools than the young and foolish. Keep us when we come to die, lest, at the very end, we would deny You! Keep us living, keep us dying, keep us laboring, keep us suffering, keep us fighting, keep us resting, keep us everywhere, for everywhere we need You, O our God!

```
Y L U K E W A R M O P A S S I O N S E W
H X K J U L B W G Y F I G H T I N G S P
B K W D J C O N I C O O G E I C C W H R
S O U N D I N F A I T H C Q G A B O I I
R I F O H A M B A S S A D O R S O N N D
E N N H N X V G V P Y R L F T N D E E E
S D O I L V V N C Y M R F C Y S R E S D
T W G N L W K D S P L N I B O T Q R K Z
I E N I I F L N I T F A Y N L D J V J Y
N L D E V F S R T H G Z B D C C T D H Z
G L J D H U Y K Y D P H F O Z E H N X H
W I T H D R A W N D M L Y N R H S K Y L
C N G A E Z B F Z Y K T U O W I G B L B
B G J T N O B M B K F Q L T E O N B M O
V W I S D O M J G F T X N T L M C G E R
V O E L G A E H E Z E K I A H I I V P R
Z H O B S C B M D T F K C K Z K G G S O
W A Y C B B E U E C A M R E E B P H Z W
M W X B A B Y L O N L Z N H S P F Y T Y
N F H L I A Q H U M B L I N G H A N D O
```

AMBASSADORS	PRINCES	BABYLON	WONDER
HEZEKIAH	PRIDE	WITHDRAWN	LUKEWARM
SOUND IN FAITH	BORROW	LIGHT	SHINES
DO NOT TAKE	INDWELLING	HUMBLING HAND	PASSIONS
WISDOM	LABORING	FIGHTING	RESTING

203

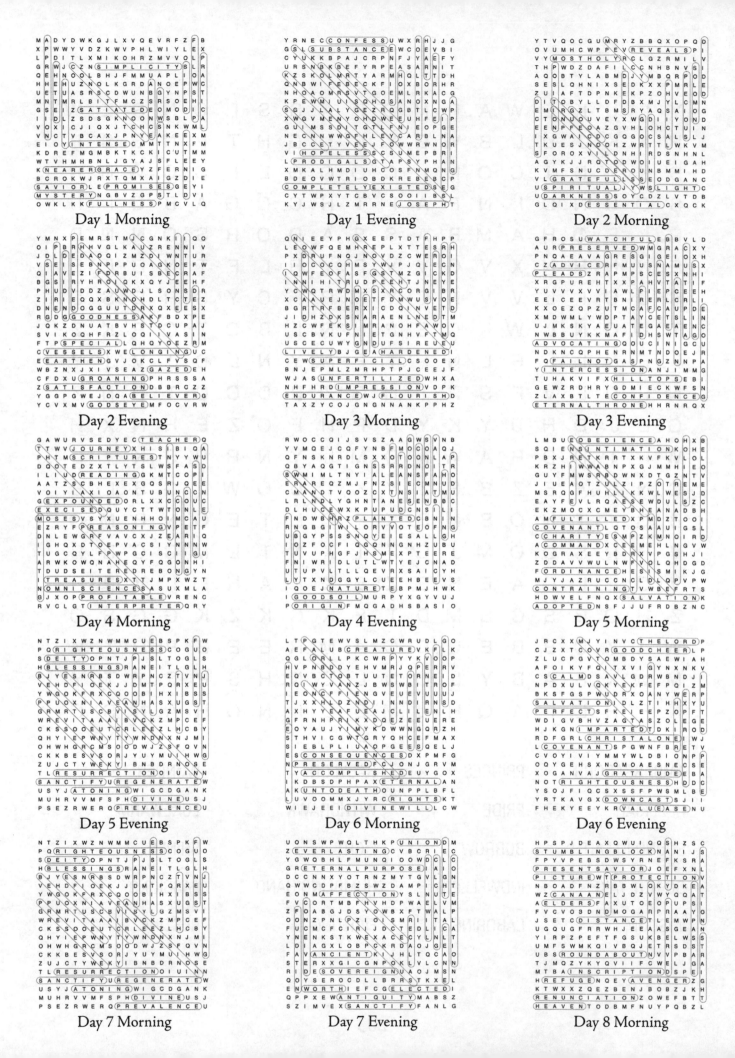

Day 1 Morning

Day 1 Evening

Day 2 Morning

Day 2 Evening

Day 3 Morning

Day 3 Evening

Day 4 Morning

Day 4 Evening

Day 5 Morning

Day 5 Evening

Day 6 Morning

Day 6 Evening

Day 7 Morning

Day 7 Evening

Day 8 Morning

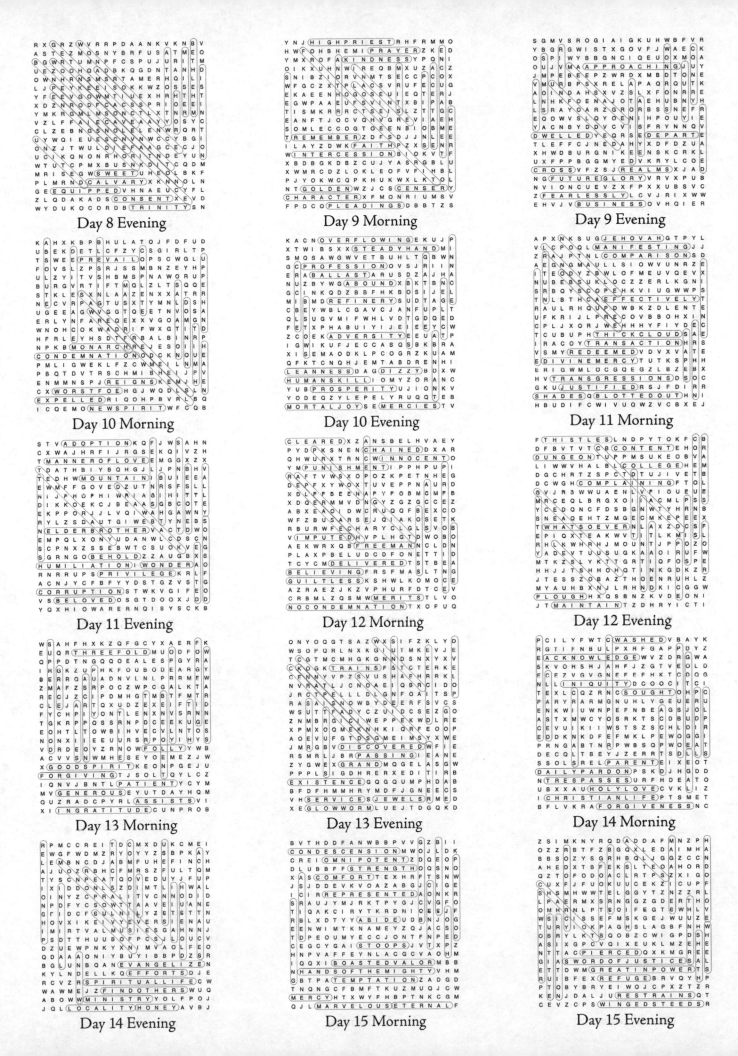

Day 8 Evening

Day 9 Morning

Day 9 Evening

Day 10 Morning

Day 10 Evening

Day 11 Morning

Day 11 Evening

Day 12 Morning

Day 12 Evening

Day 13 Morning

Day 13 Evening

Day 14 Morning

Day 14 Evening

Day 15 Morning

Day 15 Evening

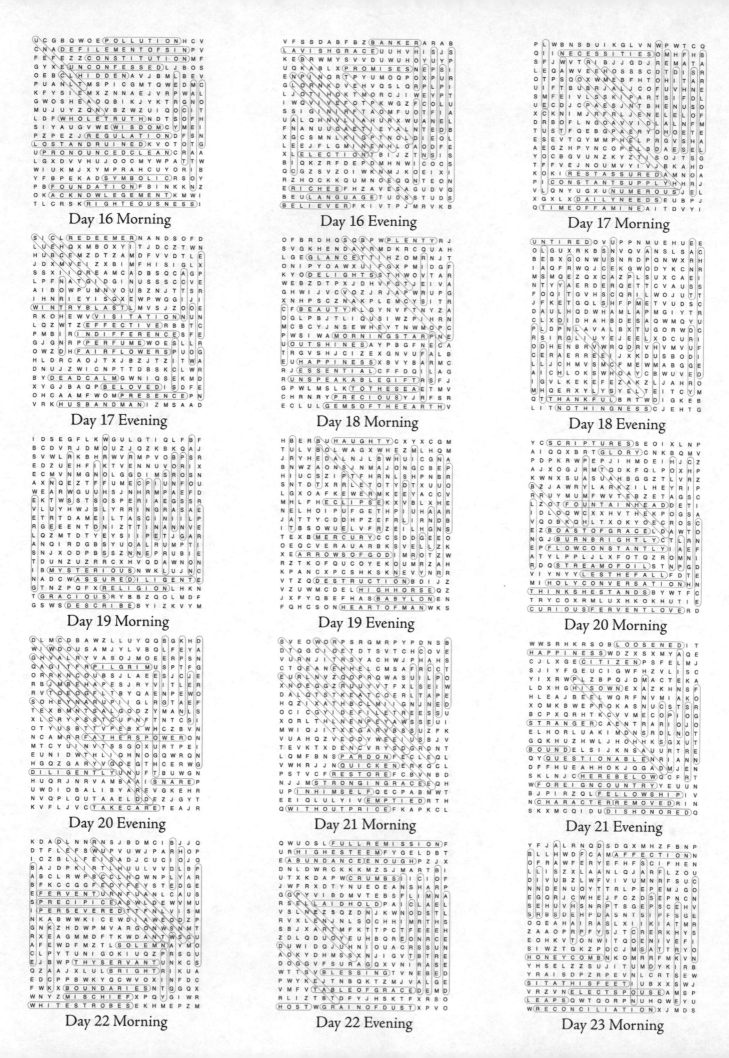

Day 16 Morning

Day 16 Evening

Day 17 Morning

Day 17 Evening

Day 18 Morning

Day 18 Evening

Day 19 Morning

Day 19 Evening

Day 20 Morning

Day 20 Evening

Day 21 Morning

Day 21 Evening

Day 22 Morning

Day 22 Evening

Day 23 Morning

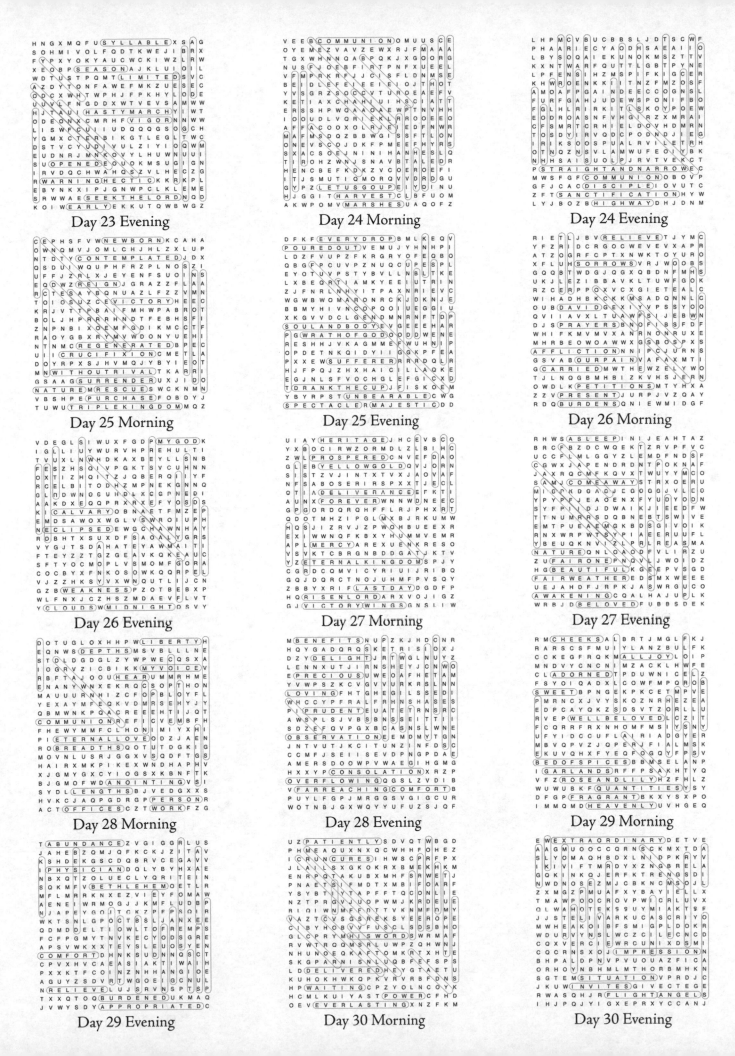

Day 23 Evening

Day 24 Morning

Day 24 Evening

Day 25 Morning

Day 25 Evening

Day 26 Morning

Day 26 Evening

Day 27 Morning

Day 27 Evening

Day 28 Morning

Day 28 Evening

Day 29 Morning

Day 29 Evening

Day 30 Morning

Day 30 Evening

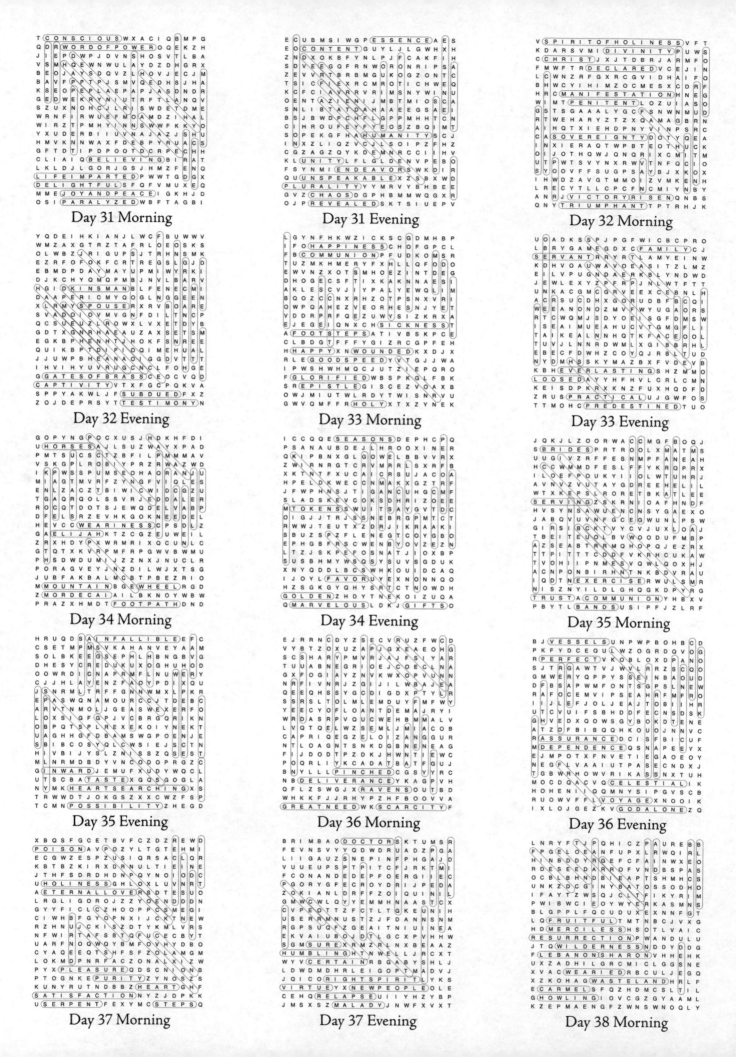

Day 31 Morning

Day 31 Evening

Day 32 Morning

Day 32 Evening

Day 33 Morning

Day 33 Evening

Day 34 Morning

Day 34 Evening

Day 35 Morning

Day 35 Evening

Day 36 Morning

Day 36 Evening

Day 37 Morning

Day 37 Evening

Day 38 Morning

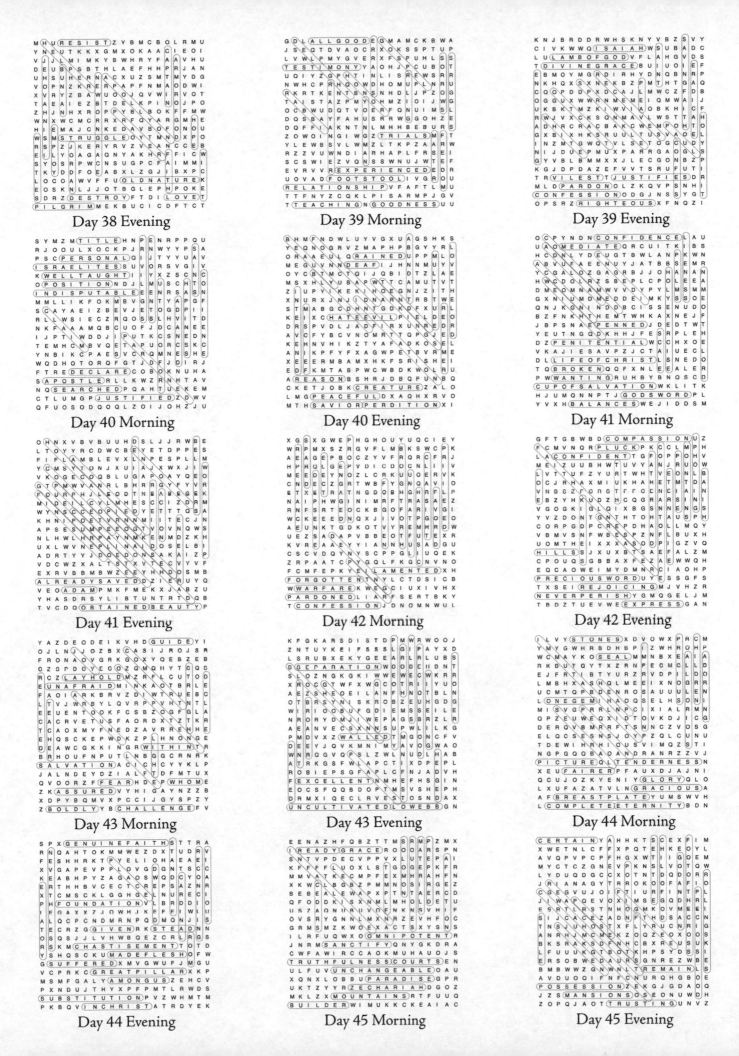

Day 38 Evening

Day 39 Morning

Day 39 Evening

Day 40 Morning

Day 40 Evening

Day 41 Morning

Day 41 Evening

Day 42 Morning

Day 42 Evening

Day 43 Morning

Day 43 Evening

Day 44 Morning

Day 44 Evening

Day 45 Morning

Day 45 Evening

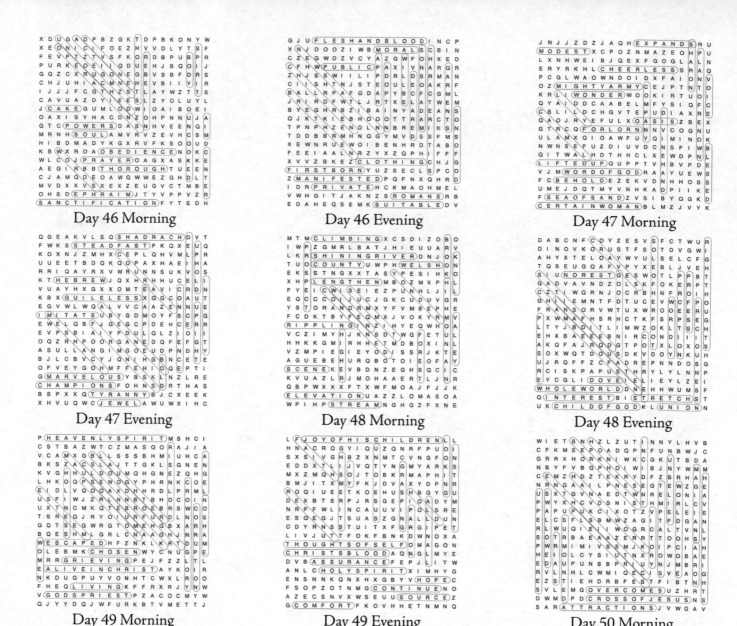

Day 46 Morning

Day 46 Evening

Day 47 Morning

Day 47 Evening

Day 48 Morning

Day 48 Evening

Day 49 Morning

Day 49 Evening

Day 50 Morning

Day 50 Evening